I0407370

The No-Nonsense Guide to Earthquake Safety

Jeffery D. Sims

Books may be purchased by contacting the publisher and author at Lulu.com, Amazon.com, or contact the author at:

Beyond The Spectrum Books
http://beyond-the-political-spectrum.blogspot.com/

The No-Nonsense Guide to Earthquake Safety
Cover Design: Jeffery D. Sims
Publisher: Lulu Books & Beyond The Spectrum Books
ISBN: 978-1-312-27410-5
1. Reference 2. Science 3. Earth Sciences 4. Safety 5. Geology 6. Earthquakes
First Edition
Printed in North Carolina, USA

Acknowledgement

For anyone and everyone who believed in me (a short list to be sure)

Table of Contents

Introduction

Simply put, in some ways I was a normal child while in other ways, I was anything but. It is the abnormal part of my being which accounts for why you are holding this book in your hot little hands (or reading it on your tablet). While I enjoyed watching cartoons, reading comic books, and favored science-fiction (notice a pattern?), I was also fascinated—infatuated actually—with learning about strange, unusual, and otherwise unexplained uncommon events. Whether the subject was verifying the legitimacy of alleged occurrences explored in the field of parapsychology, learning about what things exist beyond the boundaries of our planet through the area of astronomy, or—of relevance to you the reader—understanding the causes of interesting weather phenomenon like tornadoes and hurricanes.

As an adult, my love of learning had grown to encompass many other subjects, including history and politics (which I went to college to study). I had come to the awareness that I had/have an innate thirst for knowledge, about everything around me. As a result, I have more books than I will ever read, probably more than the average person. I've also probably had more different types of jobs than the average person. I've done a great deal of living. And in everything I've read, done, and observed, I've taken a great deal of awareness about life and the nature of the universe around us with me (yes, I know...a little grandiose, if not self-centered-sounding). I suppose by way of osmosis, I had also developed a love of teaching after having fallen into the vocation of substitute and adult education instructor. Because of these experiences, I have been driven to observe the world with an attempt to gain a deeper meaning of it all...and maybe bring a little bit of insight to others.

I am also driven to write about my observations –without the latent bias of emotion, beliefs, or cultural beliefs—in order to convey a semblance of truth (the "teacher" in me I suppose) and maybe give others a little something to think about. This is why I started blogging and writing regularly some years ago. In an indirect way, writing is also a way for me to help others to think about and offer possible solutions to grander problems posed by counterproductive policies and our own individual thinking. But it was only recently that I was motivated to combine my proclivity for (objective) observation, thirst for learning, and ultimately my writing to create a series of books based on my own intellectual curiosities and love for seeking solutions to existing problems.

This resulting compendium of interests and ideas has the (intended) benefit of imparting in those who chose to purchase and read it a level of awareness and knowledge about the an aspect of the dangers –those presented by the earth we live on—inherent in the world around us. And although there are no certain safe places to hide from real-life dangers, there *are* places as well as courses of actions that one can take to limit exposure to these dangers. I acknowledge this fact throughout the book(s) by using terms like *relatively*, *comparatively*, or variations of such words to convey that the suggestions offered are in, all likelihood based on research and other findings, the best options given the dangers and circumstances.

It is my hope that the information in this book (or as I call it, "safety manual") will save a life, or at least prevent serious injury to those who would might be affected by a related dangerous experience.

So without further ado, I present to you, the No-Nonsense Guide to Earthquake Safety...

Earthquakes

What Are They?

Earthquakes are perhaps the most largely misunderstood —and arguably—the most frightening of all natural disasters. This is no doubt due to the fact that the ground itself is considered to be the most stable of all things, and to have it become so unstable at times flies in the face of reason. And despite modern science's ever-growing ability to explain the somewhat complex causes and frightening effects of quakes, they remain completely unpredictable—adding an even more terrifying aspect to this threat.

Simply put, earthquakes are the result of geological shifts among intersecting masses of large sections of earth that occurs deep within the planet. This shifting creates "ripples" or *seismic waves* (heavy vibrations that move through the earth) that radiate upward and outward, resulting in a violent shaking of the ground which can cause poorly-constructed houses to crumble, entire buildings to collapse, roads and bridges to cracks, and people to be crushed under tons of resulting rubble.

Additionally, earthquakes can directly trigger—or be triggered by—other (related) and equally destructive events. And the accompanying destructive effects (or causes) of earthquakes can increase the potential for death and destruction far beyond that of the quake itself. To be sure, whenever the very ground starts to shake, it's almost assured that panic will ensue. But as with any natural disaster, understanding the *how's* and *why's* of the circumstances gives one an edge in being able to face, with an increased sense of confidence, most dangers presented by these particular disasters.

Damage from the May 12th, 2008 earthquake in the Sichuan province of China. The earthquake resulted in an estimate 70,000 deaths, with many more made homeless by the damage it caused.

And although there are no guarantees of survival with any such event, earthquakes are among the most survivable of natural disasters—especially if time is taken to understand this phenomenon.

How Do They Form?

To understand how and why earthquakes create the amount (and particular level) of damage that they do, its first necessary to understand how and why they occur. To begin, know that the earth is a sphere (ball) comprised of 4 distinct physical layers. The first of these layers—beginning from the innermost part of the planet—is the *inner core* located at the molten center[1] of the earth. The core is composed of molten iron ore and rock. The second layer of earth surrounds the molten core; this layer is called the *outer core*. The outer core, like the inner core is likewise heated but, only semi-molten. This is to say that this layer is heated, but not to the extent of the inner core. Closer to the surface, but still deep underground (from 5 to 20 miles, or 8 to 32 kilometers below the surface) is the *mantle*. The mantle is the largest layer of the interior of the earth, measuring some 1,800 miles (2896 km) thick. This layer of rock is semi-fluidic, and has the consistency of asphalt under the heavy weight of the earth. The semi-fluidic nature of the mantle is due to great temperature differences from the heat of the lower layers of the inner earth to that of the relative cooler temperatures found at the earth's surface. The last, outermost layer of earth, which sets atop of the mantle is what's known as the earth's *crust*.[2] The earth's crust is located just beneath where the surface land of the earth lies. Taken together, the land,

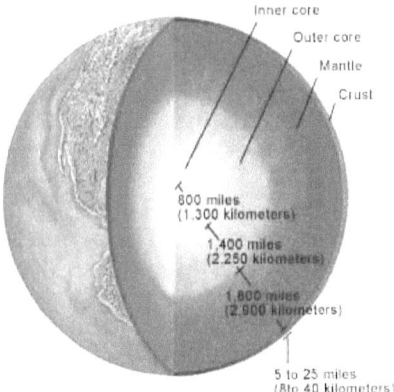

the crust, and the very outer mantle make up the surface of our planet. However, the surface—especially the layer of the outer mantle—is not made up of a single piece of contiguous planetary

---

[1] The reason the earth's core is molten is due to the pressure found at the earth's center caused by the weight the earth at this depth. This extreme pressure creates heat on the order of magnitude that is capable of heating the earth's mostly iron core along with surrounding rock.

[2] The earth's crust is very thin in comparison to the other three layers of earth. The variation of its depth comes from the differences in the beginning of the crust at the surface and the crust underneath the oceans, which is deeper. The crust is only about 3-5 miles (8 kilometers) thick under the oceans (ocean crust), and about 25 miles (40 km) thick under the continents (continental crust).

Cutaway view of the earth, illustrating the manner in which the tectonic plates that make up the geological boundaries of the continental land masses of the earth. Along the boundaries of these land mass plates are where earthquakes tend to occur, due to the "settling" of the plate masses at these points.

material. Instead, this thickened layer of the earth's surface is made up huge interconnected segments of earthen *tectonic plates*. Similar to the pieces of a puzzle, tectonic plates make up the shape of the various continents and cover the surface of the entire earth.   The points where these plates' edges intersect are called *plate boundaries*. These plate boundaries are where earthquake *faults* are located. Earthquake faults are the points within the earth where displacement of the earth along tectonic plates occurs (on the surface of the earth proper, earthquake faults may show up as a "fault line," which is the surface trace of the earthquake fault underneath the earth).

The non-contiguous nature of the Earth's surface, combined with the semi-fluidic nature of the lower mantle causes tectonic plates to occasionally move around, sliding past and bumping into each other along their edges (or fault lines). Since the edges of the plates are rough, they tend to become lodged alongside each other while the rest of the plate continually moves. Finally when the plate has moved far enough, the plate edges may become dislodged along one of the fault lines, resulting in a grinding of the land masses at a point known as the *hypocenter* (or "point of focus"). This grinding (or "settling") along the fault lines results in the release of stored energy that radiates outward in all directions, in much the same way that waves move through the water when a rock is tossed into a pond. At the surface, this energy radiates away from the *epicenter* in the form of *seismic waves* (ground vibrations) that travel across the earth faster than a bullet. Below the surface, these seismic waves are what cause the ground to rattle (shake) as they travel through it. And when these waves reach the earth's surface from the

Hypocenters vs. Epicenters

The **hypocenter** of an earthquake, located within the depths of the earth, is the point of focus at which the slip of an earthquake begins. The **epicenter** is the point on the Earth's surface directly above the hypocenter.

point of focus, the earth "quakes" in the familiar way that we know of when earthquakes occur.

Scientists have identified two individual groups of seismic waves that occur at the earth's surface; **surface waves** and **body waves** (the latter of which you will read about on page 27). Each of these wave types are made up of two subset types of seismic waves. Surface waves are made *Love waves* and *Rayleigh Waves*. These unique types of surface seismic waves are distinguished by their [relative] slow-moving and powerful natures. Love waves are the fastest travelling of the two types, moving horizontally through the earth. The result is that Love waves cause the ground to move in a side-to-side motion during a quake. At almost the same time, *Rayleigh Waves* move through the earth vertically, causing the ground to move in a "rolling" fashion similar to that observed on an ocean. Rayleigh waves are the cause of most of the shaking experienced during an earthquake, as they are much larger in amplitude (size) than other wave types that are present. Resulting from the presence of these waves within the earth's crust (i.e., outermost layer closest to the surface) as well as their unique characteristics, the worst earthquake damage is primarily (but not exclusively) found near the epicenter of these events.

The size, strength, and level of destruction that an earthquake exhibits are dependent upon several variables, both objective and subjective. Scientifically-speaking, earthquakes are measured in terms of *magnitude*, which refers to the amount of energy released at their source (hypocenter). The level of energy released by force of [the] grinding tectonic plates translates into seismic vibrations. These vibrations emanate from the point of focus in varying degrees; some earthquakes generate very small waves whereas others might produce large waves. It is the force of these seismic waves by which scientists are able to measure the magnitude of earthquakes, and rate them according to the level of expected (and observed) damage in areas near and around a quake's epicenter.

An earthquake's magnitude is determined from readings taken from vibration-sensitive instruments called *seismographs*. Because seismographs are sensitive and react to the presence of seismic waves, they are often able to detect, amplify, and record ground vibrations too small to be perceived by human beings. These readings are then translated into a corresponding numerical value which reflects strength of the waves (and their potential for creating damage in the affected areas). This measurement of earthquake magnitude is called the *Richter scale*.

Created by the American *seismologist*[3], Charles F. Richter in 1935, the Richter scale is a measure of the largest seismic wave recorded on seismographs. These wave recordings express an earthquake's magnitude in whole numbers and decimal fractions, with the whole number representing increasing levels of overall earthquake strength by factors of 10. For example, an earthquake with a rating of 3 on the Richter scale is approximately 10 times as powerful as an earthquake with a rating of 2, and a quake rated 5.4 is 11 times greater than a 4.3, and so forth. Ominously, the scale has no upper limit and generally ranges from 1 to 9; theoretically, there should never be an earthquake much above magnitude 9 on the Richter scale anywhere on Earth simply because it would require a fault larger than any on the planet[4]).

---

[3]Seismologists are scientists who study earthquakes and related plate tectonic dynamics.

[4]Although earthquakes above a measured magnitude of 9.0 are rare, they do occur albeit infrequently. The largest earthquake ever recorded was of a magnitude 9.5 that occurred in Chile in 1960. Another rare 9.0 + earthquake occurred in 1964 in Alaska (magnitude 9.2). The last recorded earthquake with at least a 9.0 magnitude measurement occurred off the coast of the island of Sumatra, Indonesia in December of 2004.

Additionally, another type of scale is often utilized in measuring an earthquake's *intensity*.[5] This scale, known as the *Modified Mercalli Intensity Scale*, was created by Italian volcanologist and seismologist Giuseppe Mercalli in 1902 to specifically measure the intensity (see footnote) of seismic activity. Similar to the Enhanced Fujita Scale used in tornado assessments, the Mercalli Scale measures damage in subjective descriptions that cannot be quantified by scientific instruments. The intensity of an earthquake is typically measured by inspectors who survey damage, and solicit questionnaires to those impacted by the event. Such observations and responses are applied to the scale to give the earthquake a rating anywhere from 1 to 12 (however, Mercalli Scale ratings are always expressed in Roman Numerals, from I - XII). For example, a tremor that makes lights swing from ceilings is ranked as a "II" (2), while a quake that forces the ground to buckling into waves, smashing everything around, ranks as a "XII" (12).

Modified Mercalli Scale vs. Richter Scale

I. Instrumental	Not felt	1-2
II. Just perceptible	Felt by only a few people, especially on upper floors of tall buildings	3
III. Slight	Felt by people lying down, seated on a hard surface, or in the upper stories of tall buildings	3.5
IV. Perceptible	Felt indoors by many, by few outside; dishes and windows rattle	4
V. Rather strong	Generally felt by everyone; sleeping people may be awakened	4.5
VI. Strong	Trees sway, chandeliers swing, bells ring, some damage from falling objects	5
VII. Very strong	General alarm; walls and plaster crack	5.5
VIII. Destructive	Felt in moving vehicles; chimneys collapse; poorly constructed buildings seriously damaged	6
IX. Ruinous	Some houses collapse; pipes break	6.5
X. Disastrous	Obvious ground cracks; railroad tracks bent; some landslides on steep hillsides	7
XI. Very disastrous	Few buildings survive; bridges damaged or destroyed; all services interrupted (electrical, water, sewage, railroad); severe landslides	7.5
XII. Catastrophic	Total destruction; objects thrown into the air; river courses and topography altered	8

Although most earthquakes occur in well-established zones of high seismic activity along tectonic plate faults (known as *interplate earthquakes*), there are a few rare instances when earthquakes occur outside of these areas. These rare *intraplate earthquakes* are quakes that happen in the interior areas of the tectonic plates—away from established (and active) plate boundaries—where the plate tends to be weaker due to its composition of softer rock. Because the interior of a tectonic plate tends to be less active in terms of seismic action, intraplate earthquakes tend to be smaller in magnitude. Seismologists theorize that intraplate quakes may be caused by strains put on plate interiors by changes in the surrounding rock. These changes are thought to be brought on by, among other suspected factors,

---

[5] Earthquake intensity refers to subjective rubric-based observations of an earthquake's impact on an affected area in terms of damage to buildings and infrastructure.

temperature and/or pressure changes, or strains whose origins may be a plate boundary some distance away.

Earthquakes can also be the result of (or the mechanism for) other phenomenon either directly or indirectly related plate tectonic activity. One of these earthquake-triggering phenomena are volcanic eruptions. Because volcanic activity tends to occur in and around earthquake-prone plate boundary zones, one event can often precipitate or even be triggered by the other[6]. In the case of volcanoes being a causal agent for earthquakes, active volcanic activity underneath the earth can produce stress changes in solid rock as *magma* (molten rock) is either injected or withdrawn from surrounding rock. If magma is removed from one area, rock begins to move in to fill the void left by the absence magma, creating tectonic pressure. If magma is injected into these unstable rocky regions, similar pressure changes during the unsteady transport of the magma can also occur. The result is a volcano-triggered (or "volcano-tectonic") earthquake.

A cutaway of a tectonic plate illustrating the interrelated relationship between volcanoes and earthquakes based on underground magma flows near plate boundary regions (where many active volcanoes are located).

Lastly and more recently, many scientists have begun to accept the possibility that some smaller earthquakes have been caused by manmade activity, especially activity linked to the exploration and extraction of oil and gas resources from underground sources. The general belief is that drilling and the related practice of *hydraulic fracturing*[7](known as "fracking") alters geological pressure points and causes shifts in the earth. An example of this phenomenon involves a series of small earthquakes in and around the city of Youngstown, Ohio in 2011. Prior to the period when the earthquakes began, the area had never previously experienced an earthquake of any measurable level. But in December of 2010, industrial projects came online across the state line in nearby Pennsylvania. During the next year, seismic instruments recorded some 109 small earthquakes in and around the Youngstown area—with the strongest measuring a magnitude of 3.9. In December of 2011, drilling operations were halted. Similar occurrences were also noted around fracking sites in both Oklahoma and Texas—with each

---

[6]For more information the symbiotic (interrelated) relationship between earthquakes and volcanoes, see the section of the book "Where Do Earthquakes Occur?"

[7]Hydraulic fracturing—"fracking"—is a process by which oil companies seek to extract oil and natural gas. The process involves injecting water, sand and other materials under high pressure into a well to fracture rock. This then creates and opens up underground fissures that assist in the free flow of these fossil fuels from these openings, which is then extracted for processing.

experiencing groups of similarly small earthquakes. This latter point highlights a particular aspect of tectonic earthquakes; that they tend to sometimes occur in "swarms" or *clusters*. This is to say that when an earthquake occurs, it tends to put a geological strain on surrounding faults. These additional strains can increase the likelihood of additional "slippage" among plate sections along the surrounding fault region, causing other smaller (or larger) related earthquakes. The result is an *earthquake cluster*, a series of high-activity seismic events related stresses places on tectonic plates.

Earthquake clusters are often classified in two different types of events. The first type of cluster is those associated with seismic activity over a given (but undefined) period of time. These *earthquake swarms* tend to be composed of smaller earthquakes, similar in magnitude, and occurring in or around the same region. Individual quakes comprising a swarm tend to range from 2 through high 4's on the Richter scale, but can occasionally go higher. In August of 2012, an earthquake swarm occurring in a region of Southern California caused an area around Imperial County to experience some 300 minor earthquakes—all in a single day! During this particular series of seismic events, the highest magnitude event was reported to have registered 5.5.[8] The following day, the same region experienced a significant lesser amount of tremors (about 100). What's more, the number of tremors and individual quakes comprising a swarm are not limited to a high concentration over a short period of time. Swarms can also occur in much smaller numbers, but over an extended period of time, such as weeks, months, or even years. An earthquake swarmaround Nagano, Japan began in August 1965, and did not subside until 3 years later, after the swarm's first tremor began.

The second type of earthquake cluster involves seismic activity associated with a major earthquake (those of a magnitude 7 or higher on the Richter scale). Major earthquakes will occasionally be sandwiched by smaller tremors that could, in themselves be considered smaller earthquakes. In such seismic events, areas that experience higher magnitude quakes also usually experience *aftershocks*—smaller earthquakes or tremors that occur in the same general area in the aftermath of a stronger quake. Aftershocks can linger in duration for a period of days, weeks, or even years following a larger quake (or the "mainshock" in this latter version of an earthquake cluster). And the strength of an aftershock is dependent upon the strength of the main shock. If an aftershock is stronger than the main shock, it is re-designated as the "mainshock" or earthquake proper. Most aftershocks tend to occur on the same fault as the mainshock tremor. However, nearby faults and fault extensions near the main shock fault will also occasionally produce aftershocks. As a matter of record, shallow earthquakes tend to produce more aftershocks than those whose hypocenters are deeper within the Earth.

Additionally, major earthquakes, can be preceded by *foreshocks*. Foreshocks are smaller earthquakes or tremors that precede larger earthquakes/main shocks in the same location. But earthquake clusters in and of themselves possess an element to their nature that makes them fully difficult to understand. This element is that scientists do not fully agree on whether smaller quakes, including foreshocks and aftershocks actually can trigger (or be triggered by) larger impending quakes.

---

[8]According to most seismologists, earthquakes of lower magnitudes—those between 1 and 2.9 on the Richter scale—are usually not felt by most humans. In the event of a higher magnitude level 2 (e.g., those 2.9), these "tremors" might be felt if they occur near a major population center, and if they occur in shallow ground. Quakes of a higher magnitude starting with 3 will, in all probability, be noticed if they occur in the vicinity of populated centers. During the August 2012 Southern California earthquake swarm, many of the smaller scale tremors could only be registered by seismographs. At one time, it was thought that earthquake swarms were limited mostly to volcanic-tectonic-related activity. However, subsequent research and observations have dispelled this notion. In fact, many earthquake swarms have been correlated to coincide with hydraulic fracturing-related activity.

Simply put, in some instances they may actually be a causal effect to larger quakes, while in other cases their activity may just been a serendipitous occurrence.

Finally, and although not a true earthquake in the sense of tectonic plate-related origins, a rare geological-weather-related phenomenon known as a cryoseism can often result in measurable seismic activity. Cryoseismic occurrences, also called "frost quakes" or ice quakes" have often been mistaken for minor intraplate earthquakes in that their proximity to the surface mimics the effects of small earthquakes—including seismic tremors, ground cracking, and various loud noises traced to the effects of ground fractures. These rare events occur when the ground and any rocky foundations below (such as bedrock) freezes over a brief period of time, usually when temperatures fall from above freezing to below zero. Moisture is then absorbed into the rock, resulting in the soil and surrounding ground freezing. As with most things that freeze, the soil and ground then expands, placing stress on and around surrounding areas. The infrequent result is that the increasing stress causes the soil and rock around this area to fracture in a spectacularly loud manner. This effect has often been described as being "explosive" in occurrence, shaking the ground's surface as it happens. Although ice quakes tend to release far less energy than true tectonic-based quakes, they often cause damage or significant changes to an affected area. In many cases, these events often leave deep cracks in the ground. Although cryoseisms tend to be localized events, they can (and do) result in multiple seismic tremors over a particular area. In January of 2014, areas in the state of Wisconsin in the U.S. and in the Canadian province of Quebec experienced ground-damaging ice quakes that resulted in some damage to the surrounding ground.

The specific type of ground damage resulting from an "ice quake" (cryoseism). Courtesy: Accuweather.com

For the most part, earthquakes, earthquake clusters, and—to a lesser extent—cryoseisms remain a mystery insomuch as understanding the relationship between each quake event. The scientific speculation, however, is the belief that earthquakes can occur either as singularly random events, or inter-relatedly as a cluster. In some cases, an earthquake can reduce the probability of subsequent earthquakes, while in other cases, relatively weak earthquakes can be the trigger for stronger earthquakes. This is to say that minor (or significant) magnitude seismic events can either be a part of an earthquake cluster, or trigger them; the full understanding of this pattern of seismic events is unknown. On the other hand, what *is* known is that major or catastrophic earthquakes tend to release and reduce stresses on the surrounding tectonic plate-fault areas where the fracturing occurs. The result then is that the probability of another earthquake tends to be greatly reduced. Conversely, if a tectonic plate-fault has not experienced a (significant) rupture for an extended period of time, the probability of an earthquake will likely increase. This difficult-to-grasp dynamic is known as the *earthquake-time dependency* by seismologists. What this means is that the probability of an earthquake occurring may be dependent on the time and magnitude of the previous earthquake on the same tectonic plate-fault. To reiterate the upshot, scientists are not fully able to understand what triggers an earthquake swarm... or why they particularly end.

But to those who reside in earthquake-frequent regions, the prevailing belief is that it is preferable to experience several small earthquakes than to have an absence of earthquake activity, especially for any extended duration of time. The thinking behind this is that frequent but smaller earthquakes tend release seismic energy in smaller bursts than the more powerful burst of seismic force that would be released as a result of a single huge tremor. More to this point of thought, if pressure between two opposing tectonic plates is allowed to constantly build, the sudden tearing loose of one (or conceivably both) plates is likely to result in a single violently seismic event, causing a huge shock and a big earthquake. The magnitude 9.5 of 1960—the largest earthquake ever recorded—centered in the Valdivia-Puerto Montt area of Chile is an extreme example of how pent-up energy from dormant seismic activity can literally explode in a single, violent episode. The Chelan seismic episode was so intense and powerful that its effects created a damage path that encompassed a geographic area that included not just the country of Chile itself, but portions of Japan, the Philippines, and even the West Coast of the U.S. (including the Hawaiian Islands) thousands of miles/kilometers away. The result was some 2,000 – 4,000 deaths caused by direct earthquake damage, and a tidal surge created by the quake (see the next section under "What makes Them Dangerous?").

What's more, predicting the duration and onset of an earthquake is also not within the scope of current scientific knowledge. In the event of a particular earthquake, the possibility of foreshocks and/or aftershocks is neither zero, nor 100 percent, but a matter of whatever unknown factors affects each individual quake. Smaller or larger subsequent earthquakes—as well as precursor quakes—can neither be discounted nor assured as a cause of effect of a quake in each case.

What Makes Them Dangerous?

Around the globe, earthquakes are a daily occurrence. Between 30 and 50 quakes—usually of a magnitude of 2 or lower on the Richter scale—occur somewhere on earth each day. But despite the fact that stronger earthquakes—those with a magnitude of 7 or higher—are more infrequent, *they* are the quakes that do the most damage, and cause the most deaths when they occur.[9] However, the fact that a particularly powerful earthquake even occurs should be an assumption that death and/or massive destruction of property might be the end result. In 2011, a powerful (for this particularly vulnerable section of the world) magnitude 7.2 earthquake struck a remote area of Pakistan. Because the quake's hypocenter was buried some 50 miles (80 kilometers) below the earth's surface, and its epicenter was at least 200 miles (321 km) removed from the nearest populated areas, there was no property damage—despite powerful aftershocks being felt as far away as New Delhi, India—and only one recorded casualty; a woman suffering a heart attack likely caused by fear.

Obviously, the majority of hazards stemming from earthquakes are those that occur as a result of the very ground itself shaking. When this happens, buildings and other structures can be damaged. In addition to the structural and cosmetic damage resulting from their physically molested by the ground shaking, buildings—particularly their foundations—can also be damaged when the ground where they were built upon settles to a different level in the aftermath of a quake.[10] Moreover, structures can partially sink into the ground if soil liquefaction occurs. Soil liquefaction happens when sand and/or soil become mixed with underground water during the course of seismic activity. When this mixture of soil and water gathers in abundant amounts, the ground will become soft in a manner similar to that of quicksand, thus losing its strength and its ability to support weight. If this liquefaction occurs under a building or other structure, said structure may begin to tilt, topple, or even sink into the ground by several feet/meters. Afterwards, the affected ground may begin to firm back up to its pre-earthquake stage as the disturbed groundwater now settles back down to its previous place within the ground.[11]

The second main earthquake hazard is ground displacement (actual ground movement) that happens along an earthquake fault along the surface. If a structure (a building, road, etc.) is built across a fault line, any ground displacement occurring during an earthquake could seriously damage or cause the structure to shear apart. When ground displacement happens, the potential damaging effect on buildings and infrastructure is similar to the damage that would take place under the same stresses induced by soil liquefaction. The difference is that during ground displacement, more direct tearing

---

[9]This is not to say that earthquakes of a lesser magnitude don't cause significant levels of death and/or destruction. The 2011 earthquake in Christchurch, New Zealand was recorded as a 6.3 magnitude seismic event. The quake caused between some $30 and $40 billion in damages, and resulted in an estimated 185 deaths. In 2012, 2 main shock earthquakes and a series of subsequent aftershocks were responsible for 27 deaths in and around areas in Northern Italy. The main shock quakes, as well as the strongest aftershocks were recorded to be below a 6 on the Richter scale; between 4.5 and 5.9 all told with this series of seismic events. The potential for death and damage/destruction of property and infrastructures resulting from earthquakes is based on various factors, as noted in the text.

[10] This is an example of *subsidence*, the motion of the ground as it shifts downward to a level different from that of the prior to a causal event, in this case, an earthquake.

[11] Liquefaction is a hazard in areas that have groundwater near the surface and sandy soil.

and/or shearing of a structure occurs as result of surface rupturing taking place across the fault line. Structures can also be damaged by particularly strong surface waves that make the ground lift and pitch to various degrees. Any structure in the path of these surface waves can potentially lean and/or topple from this ground movement.

The environmental damage resulting from ground displacement in the wake the of a magnitude 7.5 earthquake that occurred in August of 1959 near Yellowstone National Park, Montana. This particular example of displacement damage was the result of a landslide that destroyed a mountain highway and a nearby house.

Location

As illustrated, the *location* of an earthquake can be a primary factor in determining the extent of its effects in a particular area. More specifically, an earthquake—especially one of a "strong" or greater magnitude[12]—that occurs in a populated area or in the middle of the ocean is far more likely to increase its overall destructive lethality potential due to related factors. In populated areas of the developed world, the damage and disruption to the established infrastructure, the large number of structures susceptible to damage/destruction, and the comparatively high-density of people in cities can all combine increase the destructive effects of an earthquake. In less-developed areas, the relatively weak construction of vulnerable buildings and other structures, poor communication networks, and deficiencies in resources related to first-response and rescue apparatuses can all work to increase both the destructive and lethal effects of a quake beyond that which might take place in developed countries under similar circumstances.

---

[12]See: The Richter scale chart on page 6. Earthquakes with a magnitude of between 6 and 6.9 are rated as being a "strong" earthquake.

Depending on the location of a seismic event, an earthquake of a great enough magnitude can affect both developed and underdeveloped areas with an equal level of impact. But the movement of the ground, in and of itself, is rarely the cause of injury and/or death during a quake. In fact, most earthquake-related damage, injuries, and deaths result from collapsing walls, flying glass, and objects falling from shaking and collapsing structures. These impacts tend to be seen primarily in populated areas—hence the factor of location affecting a quake's impact. This impact that location has as a mitigating of factor of overall earthquake danger is often seen within the most active earthquake zone in the U.S., the West Coast. In 1989, a magnitude 6.9 earthquake (known as the Loma Prieta Earthquake) struck the San Francisco Bay area, killing some 63 and causing massive destruction in the region that included the collapse of a two-level section of Interstate 880 in nearby Oakland.

Rescue workers at the site of the Cypress Street Viaduct section of Interstate 880 in Oakland, California (where many deaths occurred) following the 1989 Loma Prieta earthquake

In addition to America's West Coast, other areas of the U.S. as well as other parts of the world are far more susceptible to the occurrence of earthquakes than others. In some of these high-frequency earthquake areas, higher-magnitude earthquakes are a particular concern, as they tend to occur at a higher-than-average rate than in other earthquake-prone regions. In a few of these areas, earthquakes can be an indicator of an impending volcanic eruption; this includes areas of the northwest U.S. (see the section, "Where Do Earthquakes Occur?").

Mountainous regions in active earthquake zones can create another set of particular hazards. In elevated terrain, earthquakes can trigger rock slides and/or landslides on mountains and hillsides by dislodging rocks and large segments of earth. The result is an avalanche of earthen debris that could tumble down into valleys and sweep away (or bury) everything in its path. An example of this earthquake hazard was witnessed in 1948, during a quake that occurred in a region of Peru that encompasses the higher elevations of the Andes Mountains. The magnitude 6.7 event resulted in an estimated 5,000 deaths (and 4 times as many injuries) due mostly to landslides triggered by the quake. According to reports, entire houses tumbled down hillsides while others were buried entirely.

If an earthquake occurs in an area encompassing a major waterway such as large lake or river, flooding could result. Earthquakes that occur in these areas can rupture dams and/or levees along a river, or affect the containment of reservoirs. The result would be flooding that would damage many buildings and potentially sweep away others. The 2011 earthquake that occurred in Japan's Fukushima Prefecture exemplifies how such a scenario could take place. In the 24 hours following the magnitude 9.0 earthquake, the Fujinuma Dam near the Abukuma River failed as a direct result of damage it had sustained during the quake the day before. A resulting flood damaged some homes, washed away others, and made local roads and a nearby bridge impassible with debris. Eight people were killed in the deluge.

On the opposite end of the danger spectrum, fires are also a hazard of earthquakes—particularly in developed populated areas. Fires can be started as underground gas and power lines are snapped and/or broken during ground displacement. In the case of broken gas lines, released gas can come into contact with an ignition source to trigger fires that are likely to spread quickly in debris piled containing many combustible materials. Live electrical currents fed through broken electrical lines can likewise trigger fires as they come into material, particularly those that are cloth-based. This fire threat can be exacerbated if water pipes and fire hydrants are damaged and broken, as this would hinder the possibility of putting out any potential fires before they spread out of control. In less-developed areas, scenarios such as wood- and/or coal-burning stoves falling over can be as much the source of a fire hazard as broken gas and electrical lines. Fires that erupted in the wake of the 1906 *Great San Francisco Earthquake* were responsible for the destruction of 80% of the city, and the majority of the more than 3,000 recorded deaths in the quake's wake (though by most statistical estimates, there were probably more deaths). After 3 full days of unchecked burning, 250,000 people were left homeless as a result of these earthquake-spurred fires.

Finally, areas near the ocean are of a particular concern for those residing in earthquake-frequent areas of the globe. This is due to the fact that earthquakes can and do occur in and around tectonic plate faults deep under the ocean. When this happens, seismic waves can trigger an event known as a *tsunami*. A tsunami is a giant wave (or series of waves) of water caused by earthquakes occurring in or near the ocean, ocean-adjacent (or underwater) landsides, or undersea volcanic eruptions. These waves of water are created far out in the ocean, at a point water is displaced by the sudden movement of large masses (like sections of earth broken off during tectonic plate shifting) into an area where water once occupied these spaces. These and similarly disruptive actions then create large waves in the water, which become rolling waves. These waves or "tsunami" can travel across the open unimpeded ocean at speeds of up to 500 mph (805 km/h)—about as fast as a jet airplane—towards the nearest shoreline, losing very little momentum along the way. When these walls of water approach a shoreline in the vicinity and wake of an earthquake, they often cause destruction (and death) where and when they move in, depending on their height and intensity. In December of 2004, a magnitude 9.0 earthquake centered under the Indian Ocean near the Indonesian island of Sumatra occurred. Within hours of the quake a tsunamihad formed in an area of waters radiating from the earthquake's epicenter. The killer tsunami travelled some 3,000 miles (4,800 km) from the epicenter near Indonesia to the eastern coast of Africa, slamming ashore in waves of water ranging anywhere from 50 to 100 ft (15 to 30 m) high along the coastlines of some different 11 countries in the region, washing away property, animals, and people. The result was an estimated death toll of 240,000, with an equal number rendered homeless and several thousands more missing and presumed dead; the bodies of people which were never found were presumed to have washed out to sea.

Magnitude

Naturally, the strength and intensity of an earthquake are the primary factors in the dangers inherent therein. Fortunately, the majority of the earthquakes that happen every day around the world tend to belong to quakes of the lowest magnitudes (those registering 2.5 or less on the Richter scale). This means that most earthquake tremors go unnoticed, and can only be acknowledged (i.e., recorded) by way of seismograph recordings. Needless to say, most earthquakes then do not cause any discernible damage or injuries. Still, the intensity of earthquakes varies. Some quakes are so minor that they can only be felt at the epicenter, if at all. Others are so intense that they man shake hundreds of thousands of square miles/kilometers, although these latter types are infrequent occurrences. The 1960 magnitude 9.5 in Chile was so powerful that it not only caused entire structures to collapse, but triggered a tsunami that caused deaths thousands of miles/kilometers away in Japan and the Philippines, a landslide in the nearby Andes Mountains, and even caused a volcanic eruption in the nearby Puyehue-Cordón Caulle Complex of volcanic mountains and fissures. But earthquakes do not have to be of the catastrophic (i.e., high magnitude) type to cause extensive damage. The 1994 so-called "Northridge Earthquake" in the San Fernando Valley region of the city of Los Angeles was a magnitude 6.7—more than 30 times less powerful than the Chilean earthquake more than 30 years earlier—but killed more than 55 people, and caused some $25 billion dollars in damage.

For all earthquakes, the level of damage and potential for death tends to rise with the increase in the strength of the quake (with the caveat that destructive potential for any given earthquake is also dependent upon how developed and populated an impacted area is). However, any significant earthquake can potentially cause both damage and fatalities. In January of 1993, an earthquake in South Africa registering a relatively paltry magnitude 2.7 on the Richter scale was responsible for 6 deaths.

Depth

Believe it or not, the focus of an earthquake can lie anywhere from the earth's surface to 435 miles (700 km) below the surface. As is true with distance from a quake's epicenter (across the earth's surface), the force of a quake's tremors tend to diminishes upwards from its hypocenter (point of focus within the earth itself). In short, deeper earthquakes are less damaging because their energy dissipates before it reaches the surface. Conversely, the closer to the surface an earthquake's point of focus is, the greater the impact of the energy produced in the form of seismic waves. The consequence is that the force of shaking at the earth's surface that occurs from an earthquake whose source lies at 310 miles (500 km) below the surface will be considerably less than if the same earthquake had occurred at a 12 mile (20 km) depth. "Shallow earthquakes" then—those defined as having a point of focus within 40 miles (60 km) of the earth's surface—tend to be the most damaging.

In January of 2010, a powerful magnitude 7.0 earthquake struck the Caribbean Island of Hispaniola, occupied by the nations of Haiti and the Dominican Republic. The quake's epicenter was concentrated on the Haitian side of the island, and therefore took the brunt of the catastrophic-level of death and destruction. The event destroyed the capital of Port-au-Prince, severely-damaged other nearby municipalities, and killed more than 200,000 people. According to scientists, the relative shallow depth of the Haiti quake—a pinpointed focus of 6.2 miles (10 km) below the Earth's surface—was a primary factor leading to the extent of death and destruction experienced on the island nation.

Distance from the Epicenter

As previously mentioned, earthquake damage tends to occur at levels proportionate to [the] distance from the epicenter of a quake. Typically, the closer to the epicenter of an earthquake any population center and/or manmade structures are the greater the level of destruction. Equally, the further away municipalities and their swellings are from the epicenter of a quake, the less the damage. However, the *true epicenter* of a quake will infrequently lie outside the area of greatest intensity and/or damage (where the greatest intensity and level of damage might be the result of other factors, such as the type of rock-soil combination where dwellings may be constructed atop). Speaking of which…

Local Geological Conditions

Oddly—or maybe obviously—enough, the geological differences in the soil and rocky consistencies of an area affected by earthquakes can be a major factor in how much (or how little) destruction can be wrought. This is because the varying consistencies of soil and rock properties within areas of the earth can affect both the speed and force by which seismic waves pass through a certain area of earth. As a result, seismic waves travelling through the earth will be affected in both their "behavioral" characteristics (for want of a better description) as well as the effect they will have on the area of impact. To illustrate this process, consider the fact that seismic waves tend to travel faster through harder rock than they do through softer rock and sediments such as soil and/or sand. As seismic waves pass from denser material (i.e., harder rocks) to less dense material (i.e., softer rocks or soils), the waves tend to slow down while their amplitude increases (this increase in the amplitude of the waves occurs based on the laws of physics; seismic waves expand to maintain the same level of active energy as they move through alternating densities of earth). The result is a more intense shaking of the ground in such regions than what would be experienced in regions (and in population centers) where denser rock and earth exist. In fact, the ground motion of populated centers established above soft rock and/or soil underpinnings can be more than 10 times more intense than that experienced in neighboring areas established above on more solid rocks. [13] This effect that the underlying soil and/or rock makeup has on the localized amplification of seismic waves is called the *site effect*.

As the phenomenon of site effect relates to how seismic waves travel through the varying types of earth and rock, the National Earthquake Hazards Reduction Program (NEHRP) has defined six different soil and rock types based on their shear-wave velocity in order to determine amplification effects. These earth rock and soil types include:

---

[13] In terms of the intensity of the ground motion during a quake, the same principle tends to hold true tends for effects of soil and/or sediment thickness. The deeper the soil and/or sediment layer above solid rock, the more soft soil there is for seismic waves to travel through, therefore creating stronger amplifications.

Type A, hard dense rock (e.g., igneous rock).
Type B, solid, less dense rock (e.g., volcanic rock).
Type C, very dense soil/sediment and soft rock (e.g., sandstone).
Type D, stiff soil/sediment (e.g., mud).
Type E, soft soil (e.g., artificial earthen fill).
Type F, soils requiring site-specific evaluations.

In terms of seismic wave amplification, earth-Type A has the least amplification, while earth-Type E exhibits the most. This means that areas that tend to resist earthquakes the best are those areas that have a lot of rock and highly compacted soil. These hard/dense rock-based regions resist ground shaking better, and do not break apart easily. As a result, property owners in these areas are not as concerned about structural damage during a quake. However, areas that are either artificially filled or built above loose sediment/soil deposits tend to suffer the most during an earthquake.[14] The increased effects of geology on seismic activity were observed during the 1989 San Francisco earthquake when so much of the city's Marina District was damaged during the event. The particularly violent ground shaking that occurred during the quake caused some of the ground underneath the Marina to liquefy. As a result, many structures lost their foundation and sank into the ground. The reason that such a high-level of destruction was visited upon the District was because the area was originally built atop weak soil and old landfill used to convert low and waterlogged marshlands into livable space. The 1989 quake illustrates those areas of land composed of comparatively weak and/or soft rock, deep sand/soil sediments, very wet, refilled, or artificially-filled earth will usually suffer the most damage during an earthquake.

Site effect is also, in large part the reason why some areas a great distance away from an earthquake can experience some level of measurable—either by people or instruments—seismic activity. The relative effects of earthquakes in the western U.S. compared to the Central or Eastern U.S. can also be linked to differences in ground softness east and west of the Rocky Mountains. For example, tremors from the historically destructive magnitude 7.8 San Francisco Earthquake of 1906 were felt as far as 350 miles (563 km) away in the middle of the then-sparsely populated state of Nevada. By contrast, the tremors emanating from the epicenter of the strongest of the 1811-12 New Madrid Earthquake Cluster was felt over 1,000 miles (1,609 km) away in Boston, Massachusetts.[15] The takeaway then is that the more condensed and compact the soil—and the more hardened rock that the soil contains—the less likely the soil will conduct seismic vibrations through areas exhibiting these particular geological structures. But the more loosely compacted the soil is in a given area, the more likely that

---

[14] Areas typically representing earth-Type E characteristics include deep valleys and areas of land where sedimentary basins (those composed of deep and loose soil). These areas are prone to increased ground motions (i.e., shaking) during an earthquake as a result of their lower altitudes. Cities built in valley basins can potentially experience earthquakes that can have a particularly catastrophic destructive and deadly impact on both their infrastructures and populations.

[15] The 1811-12 New Madrid Earthquake Cluster was a series of powerful earthquakes and intense aftershocks that struck a region of the Eastern United States along the seismically-active New Madrid fault line. This active fault borders an area where the geographic regions of 4 states –Northeast Arkansas, Northwest Tennessee, the extreme southern tip of Illinois, and the extreme southeast corner Missouri (near the city of New Madrid, hence the fault's name)—intersects. The largest of these earthquakes, estimated to have been between magnitudes 7.7. and 8.0 remain the largest and most powerful seismic events ever to take place in the Eastern half of the country.

such areas of earth will conduct seismic waves. This means that regions composed of loosely-packed soil and relatively soft rock foundations will experience more destructive earthquakes felt on the surface. Additionally, seismic vibrations travelling through areas where these geological features are prevalent tend to lengthen in duration, resulting in even more damage over time.

The remains of a building located in the Marina District of San Francisco following the 1989 earthquake that damaged large swaths of the city. The area was built atop landfill (used to cover over the bays and marshlands that once spanned the area of the city) which was used to accommodate the growth of the city's population during the earliest part of the 20th century. (USGS photo).

Architecture

One of the chief causes of injury and death to people during an earthquake is the hazard of collapsing structures; buildings, walls, bridges, glass windows, and other falling objects are major determinants in casualty levels. What's more, earthquake foreshocks can cause some potential structural damage while aftershocks can complete the collapse of entire buildings and that were damaged during the main quake in between.

In developed countries, large buildings and other components of their infrastructures tend to be constructed to resist the physical stresses put on them by shaking-induced by ground motions. In California for example, many buildings in around the major metropolitan areas (e.g., San Francisco and Los Angeles) are required to be constructed in adherence to local *building codes*. Building codes are codified standards for the construction of buildings and other inhabited structures as they relate to durability under certain foreseen conditions. In the case of earthquakes, many local and state building codes mandate that inhabited structures be constructed to withstand seismic-induced stresses. These stricter building codes reduce the incidence of injury and/or death in the event of strong earthquakes. This difference between lax building codes and stricter ones (with consideration for earthquake damage) can be seen in Mexico City. In September of 1985, an earthquake registering an exceptionally powerful magnitude 8.0 struck the Mexican capital, killing some 10,000 people, causing the collapse of more than

400 buildings, and resulting in $3 billion in damages. More than 25 years later in 2012, another earthquake with a lesser magnitude of 7.4 hit the city. However, the death toll, compared to the 1985 quake was only 2; one person from a heart attack attributed to the onset of the quake, and another who died as a result from injuries suffered in wall collapse. The difference in both the extent of casualties and the amount of structural damage has been attributed to the implementation of emergency building code revisions in the wake of the 1985 quake.

A portion of a 15-story apartment building in Mexico City collapsed during the 1985 earthquake. Building codes revisions adopted in the wake of that event helped the city withstand this year's strong earthquake with much less damage. (Photo: Courtesy of the U.S. Geological Survey).

In less-developed regions of the world, building codes (see page 41 for more on building codes) reflecting standards for earthquake-resistant structures tend to be more lax or even non-existent—due mostly to the lack of material resources. In such areas, even a moderate-level earthquake can result in the total collapse of structures lacking the proper reinforcement to resist seismic tremors. This is because buildings in these regions tend to be constructed of inferior materials such as unreinforced masonry and/or concrete. As such, many structures are highly susceptible to collapsing under the strain of seismic forces. And when they collapse *en masse*, the casualties can run up into the tens (or even hundreds) of thousands in the worse-case events. In December of 1909, a major magnitude 7.1 earthquake struck the southern part of Italy, affecting the island of Sicily and the Calabria and Messina regions of the country's mainland. The mass collapse of weakly-constructed homes and other buildings was the primary cause of the estimated 100,000 deaths that resulted in the wake of the disaster. In fact, so much did unreinforced and poorly-constructed buildings factor into the death toll that almost half of the people living in the region of Messina were killed due to the easily collapsible structures that dominated the villages of the region.

In many regions where limited resources and/or older structures abound, buildings do not perform (i.e., hold up) well under earthquake-induced strains. And the collapse of many of these relatively weak construction-styled buildings has caused thousands of deaths over the decades. In resource-abundant countries, strong enough earthquakes could conceivably cause just as potential havoc. However, as a general rule the more code-compliant infrastructures and available resources lend themselves to lower damage and higher death tolls. But in both developed and under-developed regions, the worst possible structure to find oneself in during an earthquake is one composed of unreinforced brick masonry. On the other hand, many buildings, particularly skyscrapers are constructed to reduce their tendency to shake during earthquake vibrations.

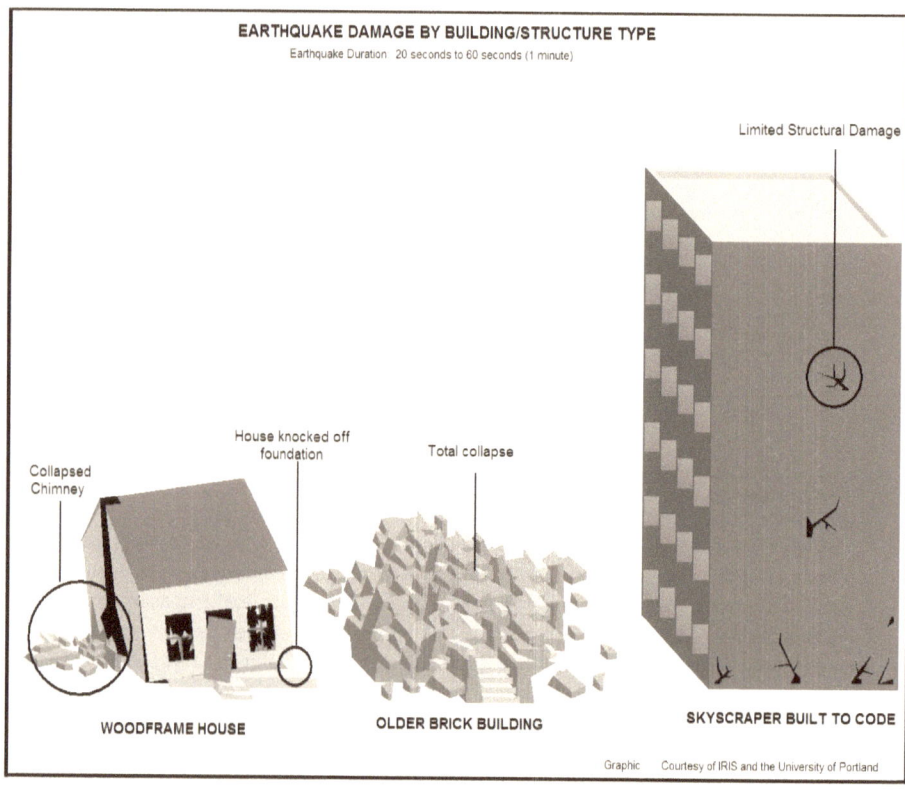

EARTHQUAKE DAMAGE BY BUILDING/STRUCTURE TYPE
Earthquake Duration: 20 seconds to 60 seconds (1 minute)

Limited Structural Damage

Collapsed Chimney

House knocked off foundation

Total collapse

WOODFRAME HOUSE

OLDER BRICK BUILDING

SKYSCRAPER BUILT TO CODE

Graphic   Courtesy of IRIS and the University of Portland

Where Do Earthquakes Occur?

As discussed earlier, earthquakes are the result of tectonic plates of the earth's *crust*—the layer of earth that includes the surface and up to 25 miles (40 km) below the surface—as they motion atop the movement of the upper *mantle* underneath the crust. Between the crust and the upper mantle, earthquakes occur within the upper levels of the earth ranging from the surface to about 500 miles (800 km) below the surface. *Earthquake faults* are the cracks in the earth where sections of a plate (or two interconnected plates) are moving in opposing directions. These faults form from the boundaries near the edges of the tectonic plates. Atop these boundary regions on the surface, earthquakes (in addition to volcanic eruptions) tend to be more frequent than in non-plate boundary areas. In the U.S. for example, areas along the West Coast (California, Washington state, and Alaska) are widely known to be the center for the majority of the earthquake activity that takes place within country.

Upwards of 95% of all the earthquakes in the world occur along active tectonic plate boundaries. The remaining 5% of earthquakes occur in areas away from these boundaries and established earthquake fault lines. And although they occur in many different regions (and countries) around the world annually, 80% of the total numbers of earthquakes that occur yearly do so in and around an area bordering the various oceanic and continental tectonic plates ringing the Pacific Ocean. If drawn on a map, this geographical area of highly active seismic and volcanic activity follows a pattern atop plate boundaries that borders the West Coast of North America, the Aleutian Island chain off the coast of Southern Alaska, the two Koreas (North and South), Japan and its environs, Indonesia, the Philippines, the Southwest coast of China, New Zealand, and finally the West Coast of the South American continent.

Within this region concentrated along the Pacific Rim, the edges of the major and minor continental and oceanic plates meet the edges of the giant Pacific Plate, which lies beneath the Pacific Ocean.[16] This region of intense tectonic activity, which forms a mapped ring around the Pacific Rim, is known as the "Ring of Fire" by scientists. Seismic (and volcanic) activity that occurs within the *Ring* causes frequent earthquakes along the West Coast of North and South America, along the ocean coasts bordering Alaska, and around the islands that make up Japan. Seismic activity within the Ring is also responsible for volcanic eruptions in the Northwest United States, in the Andes Mountains of South America, and in the Philippines.

However, earthquakes do not happen exclusively in and around this area of high seismic activity; remember 5% of the world's earthquakes occur in regions away from this plate boundary region (intraplate earthquakes). But even within this small number of off-boundary earthquakes, some areas tend to experience more quakes than others. In the U.S., the New Madrid fault area (see the footnote, page 18-19) does not lie along any of the major continental plate boundaries, but remains a moderately-active zone for seismic activity. Outside of the continental plate-bounded West Coast, this area experiences more earthquakes than any other region of the country (albeit not as frequently as the West Coast).

---

[16] Most of the world's known tectonic plates, both within this region and in other areas around the globe have been identified and named by geologists and other scientists who study earthquakes and such related phenomena (see: Page 23 for a map of these plate boundaries)

Furthermore, among the minority of earthquakes that do not occur along plate boundaries but do so within active intraplate regions are the infrequently or rare quakes that happen in unexpected areas.

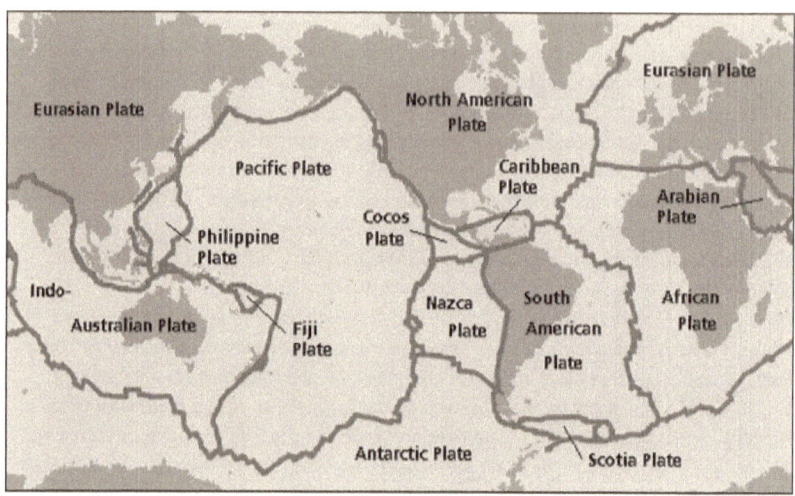

Above: A geological map of the known major and minor tectonic plate boundaries around the globe, including the largest of these plates, the enormous Pacific Plate, where the majority of the world's earthquake activity occurs. Below: Volcanic arcs and oceanic trenches partly encircle the Pacific Rim Basin to form the so-called Ring of Fire, a zone of frequent earthquakes and volcanic eruptions. Below: a map of the U.S. indicating the likelihood of earthquakes for all geographical regions based on the history of recorded earthquake occurrences.

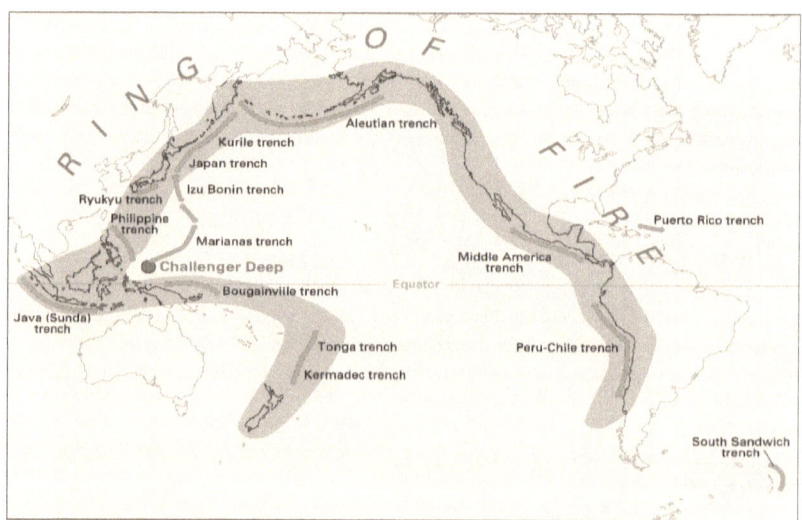

This is to say that earthquakes have occurred in areas which are neither widely known to have them, or have them so infrequently that their occurrence is considered unusual. In 2011, low-magnitude earthquakes occurred near the capital city of Canada, Ottawa (registering a magnitude 3.0), and near the cities of Jackson and Alpine in the state of Wyoming (registering 3.1 and 3.4 respectively, on consecutive days). In the same year, a moderate magnitude 5.2 quake struck the small African country of Zambia near a manmade lake.

The fact of the matter is that individuals who reside in known seismic activity zones should be aware of said reality. According to the United States Geological Survey (USGS), the scientific agency arm of the federal government responsible for studying and hazards to the country's landscape and ecosystems, the regions/states that have the highest frequency for earthquakes are as follows:[17]

1. Alaska
2. California
3. Hawaii
4. Nevada
5. Washington

In addition to these states comprising much of America's west, northwest, and Alaskan coast regions, another region of concern is the New Madrid Seismic Zone (the most active earthquake zone in the U.S. east of the Rocky Mountains) located in the middle section of the country. Whereas the overwhelming majority of earthquakes tend to occur along active fault lines around the Earth's tectonic plate edges, the active New Madrid earthquake zone represents something of a mystery in the realm of geological science. Because the very existence of an earthquake fault as active as the New Madrid defies the norm is terms of location away from plate boundaries, the destructive potential for the area of the country that could be affected by a major quake along this fault line could be enormous. During the 1811-1812 New Madrid Earthquake Cluster, an estimated (for the pre-Richter Scale era) maximum magnitude 8.0 quake—accompanied by thousands of aftershocks—struck within this seismic zone, and caused extensive environmental damage, the evidence of which still stands to this day. According to newspaper reports from the time period, the ground rose and fell by several feet/meters in several places within the affected region, trees were bent in unusually contorted manners, masonry-constructed buildings and homes were severely damaged (or completely destroyed), and entire islands within large rivers sunk underwater.[18]

The death toll from the series of quakes, although unknown, was thought to be very low due to the limited number of people that had settled in the region (which was still very much forested) prior to the

---

[17] The list of the most earthquake-prone states is based on the results of a study by the USGS of recorded and/or verifiable reports of all earthquakes taking place in the country for a period between the years 1974 to 2003.

[18] See Appendix: F for more historical background information, including documented effects, on the New Madrid Earthquake Cluster of 1811-1812.

event(s). But many scientists predict that, based on a combination of the large number of people now residing in the seismic zone and the lack of structures conforming to earthquake-resistant building codes, an earthquake of magnitudes similar to those of the 19th century cluster would cause catastrophic damage and loss of life. Although not common to the region, scientists estimate that such an earthquake (or series of earthquakes) is quite possible within the next 50 years.

In Canada, the most earthquake prone provinces/regions are British Columbia, the Yukon Territory, and—to a lesser extent—New Brunswick and Newfoundland. In the case of the latter seismically-active region, a particularly powerful 1929 earthquake centered off the coast of Newfoundland was reminiscent of the strongest of the New Madrid zone earthquake cluster. The earthquake, known as the Grand Banks Earthquake registered a surprisingly strong 7.2 magnitude—highly unusual for the region. Also like the New Madrid cluster, the 1929 Grand Banks quake caused a great deal of environmental damage, although not directly.[19] The upshot is that while strong earthquakes are relatively common along known plate boundaries, they can also occasionally strike in uncommonly active seismic regions as well.

And while it's easier to measure the occurrence of earthquakes among (and between) individual states, provinces, and regions, it's a bit more difficult to do so among the world's countries. This is because globally, there are so many more individual variables to take into account for any attempt to quantify earthquake frequency. For example, when attempting to determine just *which* particular country has the most earthquakes, the ability to record seismic events in isolated locales becomes a major factor in trying to make such a determination. For the two most earthquake prone countries in the world—Japan and Indonesia—this issue becomes most apparent. Since Japan is a highly-developed country located in a very active seismic area, it boasts the densest seismic network of any country on Earth. This means that it is very easy to record earthquakes, including most of those among the smallest magnitudes that originate within the island nation. However, because of its larger size, its decentralized geography, and the fact that the country has a limited seismic network, the number of earthquakes that occur in Indonesia in a given year is difficult to measure—despite sitting within the same general (and active) earthquake region as Japan. Overall, if we were to take a country's relative size as the chef factor in determining the number of earthquakes experienced, the Pacific island nations of Togo and Fiji would rank as having the highest number (keeping in mind that each of these countries also has sparse seismic activity networks).

Other countries notable for experiencing a high number of catastrophic earthquakes as well as the tragic corresponding factor of the highest number of deaths per major seismic episode lie within the same general region of the world—the southern and central portions of the Asian continent. These countries, China, Iran, and Turkey, all have a history of particularly devastating earthquakes within the last several centuries of record-keeping. For countries outside this region, the South American countries of Chile and Peru also tend to experience a high number of powerful earthquakes.

---

[19] The Grand Banks Earthquake was so strong that it created an underwater *slump* (a mass usually consisting of layers of rock and other sediments that moves down a slope, much like a landslide), that in turn generated a tsunami. The tsunami devastated some 40 villages on the southern coast of the nearby Burin Peninsula. Also damaged were homes on Cape Breton Island, which lay in the Atlantic Ocean in the affected zone. The island also experienced landslides, which blocked roads.

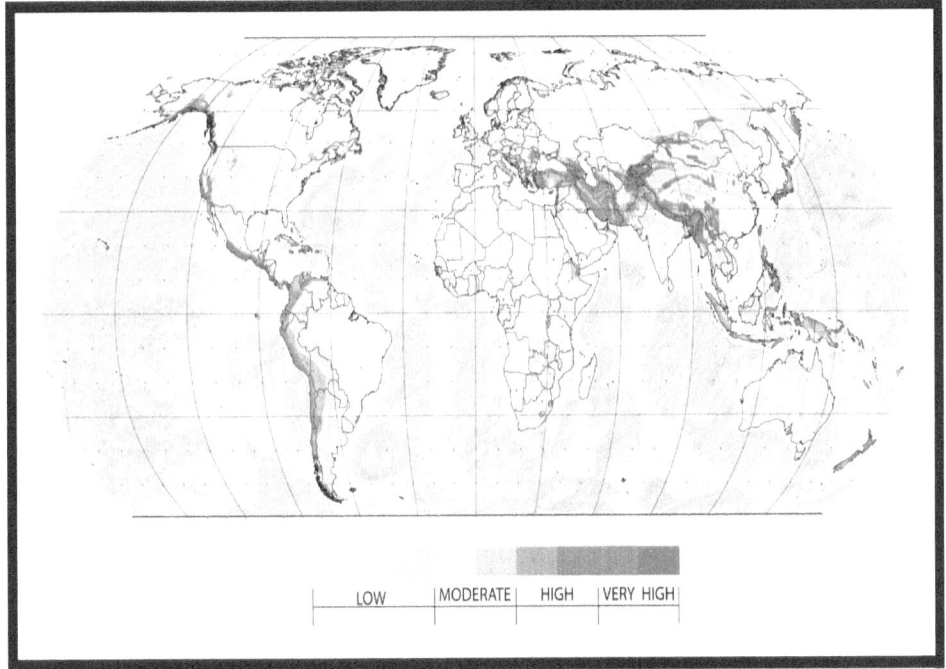

LOW | MODERATE | HIGH | VERY HIGH

A global map of the most seismically active regions in the world (indicated by the darker coloring on the map). The darker colors indicates the highest incidence of seismic activity for that region.

What to Be On the Alert for…

Strictly-speaking, there are no tell-tale changes in environmental conditions that might indicate the impending arrival of an earthquake. Unlike other natural disasters such as tornadoes or hurricanes, earthquakes tend to come on suddenly, strike with varying rates of intensity, and end just as suddenly. As this is often the case, there is no universal long- or even intermediate-range system by which people can be warned about an imminent earthquake threat (again, such as there is with tornadoes and/or hurricanes). Given our current level of understanding—or lack thereof—with regard to the science of plate tectonics, we simply cannot predict when tectonic plates will slide against one another to create the resulting event we know as earthquakes. However, some earthquake-prone countries have established seismic activity detection systems that are designed to provide a few moments of advance warning of detected earthquake-related activity for a given area. These warning systems are based on our current, albeit limited level of scientific understanding of plate tectonics and related seismic activity.

Earthquake Detection

Earthquake warning systems do not "detect" (i.e., predict) actual earthquakes per se—the anticipated slipping and grinding of fault/tectonic plates against or past each other. What they *are* designed to do is detect the generated seismic waves that emanate from geological activity within the earth. This is possible because—contrary to how it may appear on the surface—earthquakes are not exactly instantaneous occurrences. The triggering event of tectonic plate slippage triggers seismic waves. The seismic waves radiate out from a quake's hypocenter, causing damage…and what people feel when they experience the characteristic shaking. And since these waves actually *radiate* from the center of seismic activity, it takes a few moments for these waves to travel from their point of origin to the point where they cause damage to property and potentially cost the lives of those some distance away.

These detectable seismic waves are in fact the second group type of seismic waves first discussed on pages 5 and 6. Where we've learned about **surface waves** previously, the second group-type of seismic waves are known as **body waves**. *Body waves* travel through the interior of the earth and arrive at detection points before the surface waves (see pages 5-6). Body waves tend to be comprised of a higher frequency than *surface waves* (*Love waves* and *Rayleigh waves*). Like surface waves, body waves are made up of two subset wave types known as *"P"* (or Primary) *Waves* and *"S"* (or Secondary) *Waves*. P waves are fastest moving type of seismic wave and, consequently, are the first to be detected by seismic activity detectors. This is because P waves are easily able to move through most layers of earth, whether they be composed of solid rock or fluids (such as bodies or semi-solid landfill). S waves are the slower-moving seismic wave type that follows behind the front-running P wave. S waves are slower moving because they can only move through solid rock and material, and not through liquids or semi-solid mediums. S waves are what are felt during a quake; in effect, S waves are the earthquake itself.

How seismic activity detection systems work is that they detect faster-moving P waves that strike in advance of slower moving s waves. Established systems use the P wave detection to estimate the intensity of S-waves. If S waves are deemed to be sufficiently powerful, seismic sensors sends signals that trigger alarms, which send out warnings to areas that might be impacted locally by S impending waves. Depending on the distance a potentially affected population center is from the epicenter of an impending earthquake, the systems can provide limited warning to those who might be impacted to

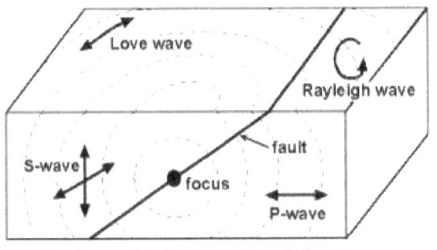

Directions of body waves (P and S) and surface waves (Rayleigh and Love) generated by an earthquake.

prepare. Such warnings can range anywhere from 10 seconds up to a full minute before an earthquake actually strikes. And because it takes longer for larger, more powerful earthquakes to spread over larger areas, the amount of warning time can be increased. The same "extended" lead warning time applies if an earthquake's epicenter is some distance away from a potentially affected region. However, if a potentially affected area is either right atop of the hypocenter, or near an earthquake's epicenter, there may be no warning delivered at all. The shaking at the epicenter occurs about a second after the P waves (not an instantaneous reaction between plate slipping and seismic wave creation, but almost immediate to be clear).

So far, the only country in the world which currently implements an operational level earthquake detection and/or warning system is Japan. After a particularly destructive earthquake in 1995, the nation of Japan invested upwards of a $1 billion in the development of an Earthquake Early Warning system (EEW). The Japanese EEW system came online in 2006 and was first implemented successfully the following year. The Japanese EEW was created based on the current level of scientific understanding of plate tectonics and knowledge of the attributes of particular seismic waves. Operated by the Japanese Meteorological Agency (JMA), the Japanese EEW system is built upon a network consisting of about 1,000 seismic wave detectors scattered all around the island nation. The Japanese EEW was first used on December 7th 2007 in response to a magnitude 7.3 earthquake that struck underwater off the nation's northwest coast. Within seconds after the first seismic waves were detected by network sensors, the EEW triggered a complex of embedded alarms that sent out a nationwide notification of detected seismic activity. Media networks—television and radio stations— immediately began issuing imminent earthquake warnings, while text messages were simultaneously sent to millions of cell phone customers in and around the capital city of Tokyo. This variable but brief of lag time between the first detectable seismic waves and the effect of seismic tremors allows for those who might live in impacted areas to take cover and/or to implement protocols that might mitigate the

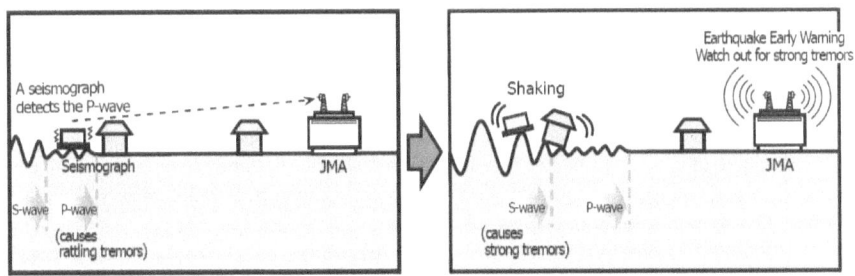

An illustration of how the Japanese Earthquake Early Warning (EEW) system works in issuing warnings for impending seismic/earthquake activity.

potential for mass casualties. In fact, some of these precautions integrated into Japan's EEW system (in addition to broadcasting warnings over media networks) include the transmission of signals which automatically shut down vulnerable computer systems, stop moving elevators at the nearest floor, and stop moving trains to prevent derailing.

Less-fully integrated EEW systems are in place —in limited operation—in other areas around the globe. Less extensive and sophisticated version of the EEW systems are in current use in and around Mexico City (the oldest of these EEW systems), Taiwan, Turkey, and Romania. As of September of 2013 in the U.S., officials in the state of California were mandating that a variation of the Japanese EEW system begin development. This initiative would include adopting comprehensive standards for any warnings issued by the system, as well as securing funding. Although a series of seismic monitors are already in place in the most

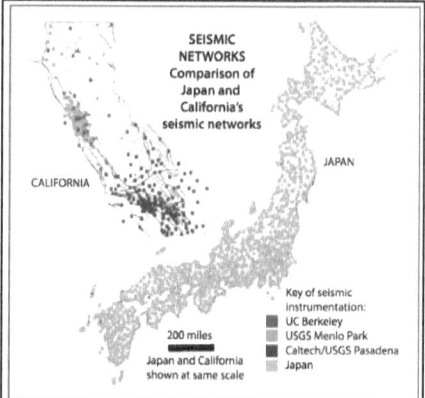

The comparative difference in seismic network sensor placement between California (the most earthquake-prone region/state in the U.S.) and Japan, the most earthquake-prone country in the world. California's seismic network encompasses approximately 600 sensors at 385 station sites what are not connected by a single unified network, as is the case in Japan. In California, seismic instrumentation gaps exist along the middle and northern San Andreas Fault Zones. Additionally, these gaps also exist within the various fault systems of the Sierra Nevada Range.

seismically-active regions of the state, the endeavor to establish a fully-integrated EEW would use the existing monitors as a starting point. This would eventually lead to upgrades to these existing monitors and the establishment of an estimated 100 new monitoring stations spread around the state. Despite both the use of the limited EEW systems already implemented in different countries and the undertaking to create a high-tech American version, it is likely to be some time before these or some other form of actual earthquake prediction can be developed. What's more, it may be even longer before any practical level of early earthquake warning system is instituted with any viable level of real-world accuracy. Still, attempts by science to understand earthquake dynamics are on-going, and most geologists feel confident that an effective system of earthquake prediction lies somewhere in the near to intermediate future. [20]

Possible Signs of an Earthquake

In the absence of proven seismic predictors that could point to the imminent arrival of an earthquake, there are many documented indications that observable, often strange environmental changes sometimes·occur prior to some earthquakes. In fact, reports of many people having observed unusual happenings in an area right before an earthquake have been documented for centuries. And despite such observations being only preliminarily scientific and anecdotal currently, reports of unusual manifestations appearing –as possible earthquake "warning signs"—continue to be documented prior to some earthquakes. Though each instance of these strange pre-quake occurrences varies in size, scope,

---

[20] See: Appendix: H, "The Future of Earthquake Prediction" for more information on the current level of progress regarding the possibility (and/or prospect) of earthquake prediction.

appearance, and duration, each manifestation has been categorized in terms of their general mode. Among these possible indicators of an earthquake are:

Foreshocks

Generally speaking, earthquakes tend to occur in clusters rather than occur as a single major seismic tremor, though this is not always so (see: page 9). But every quake is different; not all earthquake events follow the foreshock, mainshock, aftershock pattern. Sometimes there are only aftershocks following the mainshock. Sometimes, there are only groups of small tremors comprising a single seismic event. Still at other times, there are *foreshocks*—small quakes that might indicate a possible larger, more substantial event.[21] In the case of foreshocks, these smaller tremors may foreshadow an upcoming larger quake (mainshock) in the near future. However, foreshocks are extremely hard to determine in the absence of stronger quakes indicating a mainshock. But when they *can* be identified as being such, foreshocks can be used to some level of effect in providing warning of a larger quake.

On February 4th of 1975, a magnitude 7.2 earthquake struck the large city of Haicheng in China. The quake resulted in death toll of between 1,500 and 2,000 of the city's nearly 1 million residents. But the casualty rate could have still been much higher. What many considered to be a key factor in keeping the death toll from rising was the decision by local officials to initiate orders to evacuate the city in anticipation of the earthquake. This decision was reported to have been spurred by a series of strong damaging seismic foreshocks that foreshadowed a more powerful mainshock to come.

But this one and only reported case where earthquake foreshocks actually resulted in proactive responses illustrates how uncertain these particular seismic precursors are as a telltale sign of an impending earthquake. Foreshocks may or may not happen before an earthquake. Or a seismic tremor of a small enough magnitude—that under other circumstances might be considered a foreshock—may be considered an earthquake itself, provided that it isn't followed by larger magnitude quakes. Even still, quakes of equal magnitude may occur in a cluster, making it difficult to determine whether a foreshock had even occurred.[22] At any rate, it is a good practice to employ a level of vigilance when small tremors occur, particularly if they do so in seismically-active regions which haven't experienced a significant earthquake for an extended period of time. Such tremors may actually be foreshocks of a larger impending earthquake.

(Strange) Changes in Animal Behavior

Another reportedly observed, but not scientifically verified indication of an impending earthquake is a change in the behavior of animals. In fact, this particular observation goes back centuries prior to the introduction of scientific inquiry and reason-based fact-finding. Since the earliest references (from the ancient Greeks[23]) of this phenomenon, there are literally thousands—though mostly anecdotal—of

---

[21] The issue with determining the presence of earthquake foreshocks (or aftershocks for that matter) is that—unless an earthquake occurs as a stand-alone single seismic event—they can only be identified as such during a cluster event. This is to say that what marks tremors as "foreshocks" is the fact that a major or mainshock quake happens afterward. Foreshocks can only be identified as such in retrospect of an earthquake event.
[22] A year after the following the Haicheng earthquake, another even more powerful quake struck the same general region, killing an estimation of between a quarter of a million to half a million people. And although a noted Chinese scientist predicted the high likelihood of an earthquake in the Tangshan region would occur between July 22, 1976 and August 5, 1976, the quake produced no foreshocks at all.

reports of fish, dogs, bears, birds, and even insects exhibiting atypical behaviors in the weeks, days, and minutes before an earthquake. A well-documented example of this apparent phenomenon was reported in the days and weeks prior to the Haicheng earthquake, in which many of the devastated city's residents had observed indigenous snakes emerging from their burrows nearly a month before earthquake had struck the city. What made this occurrence noteworthy was that the snakes were in the midst of their hibernation period (the earthquake had occurred during the winter, when temperatures were well below freezing—and lethal to cold-blooded animals). More so, it was also reported that chickens in and around the city had, in some cases, begun flying up into nearby trees and screeching wildly. In a similar manner, in the time period prior to the 1954 7.1 magnitude Sophades, Greece earthquake, storks in the area were observed to have been flying away and exhibiting unusual behavior patterns reflective of agitation and general disturbance. And just hours prior to a July 2009 earthquake in San Diego, California, local residents living and visiting near the ocean discovered dozens of Humboldt squid washed up on local beaches (normally, this particular breed of deep sea squid found at ocean depths of between 656 and 1968 ft./ 200 and 600m). It is widely suspected that the creatures' beaching themselves was in response to the earthquake that followed later.

And because there are been so many instances of unusual pre-earthquake animal behavior on record, scientists have actually begun to take an interest in this occurrence by initiating studies. Preliminary hypotheses of this phenomenon include the speculation that some aquatic-based animals are able to sense minute chemical changes in groundwater prior to a quake. Additionally, there is further scientific suspicion that—in addition to possible changes in groundwater—animals might be capable of sensing other possible environmental precursors to an earthquake that have yet to be confirmed. Other possible precursors believed to be sensed by animals include minute ground vibrations beyond humans' ability to measure, ground tilting, and changes in electrical or magnetic fields. Yet another hypothesis related to pre-earthquake animal behavior is the speculation that different animals may in fact, be able to sense (i.e., *feel*) the seismic P waves that are produced in the minutes (or seconds) before the more powerful S wave arrives. Finally, it's also suspected that certain animals might actually be able to hear seismic activity that precedes earthquakes (i.e., the grinding and breaking of rocks, or other minute seismic rumblings taking place underground) that might occur below the threshold of human hearing. This theory might explain why dogs have been observed engaging in incessant howling and other odd behaviors before actual tremors are felt.

While some consider the link between odd animal behavior and earthquakes too tenuous to be considered as having any relevant correlation, others accept this phenomenon as having both real-world validity and application. In terms of scientific proofs, our general inability to detect the existence of measurable environmental changes that might indicate an imminent earthquake prevents us from establishing a solid link between changes in animal behaviors and quakes. Furthermore, whether or not animals are actually able to sense an impending earthquake days or weeks before it occurs is treated with a lot more skepticism within the scientific community. One reason for this skepticism is that in some cases of reported strange animal behavior, the unusual behavior is only *sometimes* observed. Also, some observations of these behaviors were noted *only* in retrospect of a following quake. On the

---

[23] The earliest known records of unusual animal behavior before an earthquake can be traced to the 4th century B.C. (373), where Greek historians observed and recorded instances where animals, including rats, snakes and weasels deserted *en masse* the Greek city of Helice several days before an extremely powerful earthquake nearly destroyed the entire city.

other hand, others have taken a keen enough interest in observing pre-quake animal behavior to base public warnings on them. Countries such as China and Japan have integrated these observations into their respective national earthquake warning systems.

While these examples of odd animal behavior can be explained away by other rational explanations outside of earthquakes,[24] it might be worth making note of any changes in normal animal behavior in earthquake-prone regions.[25]

"Earthquake Lights"

Still another rarely documented, but often reported occurrence that has actually been documented in photographs in multiple instances is the phenomenon known as "earthquake lights." *Earthquake lights* (or "earthquake lightning" as it's sometimes called) have been described as unusual discharges and/or flashes of light that sometimes appear either in the sky or near the ground before (or after) an earthquake in the anticipated affected area. These strange lights can take on various shapes and forms, and appear in many color variations. For years, individuals have reported seeing white or bright-colored flares, or floating flashing orbs, and/or rainbow-colored flickering "flames." These mostly localized fields of light have been reported appearing primarily in the sky anywhere from a few seconds to hours at a time. And just as in the many reported cases of strange animal behaviors prior to earthquakes, the history of these mysterious lights goes back several centuries. Among the most notable reported instances of this phenomenon include:

• In the aftermath of an 1888 earthquake that struck an area of New Zealand, there were multiple reports of "luminous appearances" and "an extraordinary glow" visible in the sky for several hours afterwards.

• Prior to both, the 1811-12 New Madrid Earthquake Cluster in Missouri, and the 1906 San Francisco, California, there were several reports of individuals who witnessed faint rainbows of lights in the sky in both cases.

• Earthquake lights were reported being seen during the 1930 Idu, Japan earthquake. In fact, these unusual lights were said to have been visible up to 70 miles (112 kilometers) from the epicenter of the quake

• Some 11 days before the November 1988 earthquake in the Canadian province of Quebec, a bright purple-pinkish-colored globe of light was reported moving through the sky along the St. Lawrence River Quebec City.

• In Pisco, Peru, a naval officer reported pale-blue columns of light bursting four times in succession out of the water during a magnitude 8.0 earthquake in 2007. These strange lights were captured on nearby security cameras located elsewhere in the South American city.

---

[24] It should be noted that animal (and insect) behaviors that might be considered "strange" is not always present prior to an earthquake, and therefore is hardly a certainty insomuch as predictability. During one study on animal behavior and earthquakes, ants in the Mojave Desert region of California were observed prior to anticipated earthquake activity. In June of 1992, tremors began to shake the area of the desert region. Measurements and observations made and compared before and after the quake revealed the ants failed to alter their behavior prior to or even during the earthquake—then the largest quake to strike the US in the 40-year period leading up to the quake.

[25] See Appendix: I for further information on cases involving unusual animal behavior approximating an imminent earthquake.

•Seconds before the 2009 L'Aquila, Italy, witnesses reported flickering flames of light approximately 4 inches (10 centimeters) in height high hovering just above the surface of Francesco Crispi Avenue in the town's historical city center.

Scientists—at least those who agree that these rarely-seen events are in fact real occurrences—utilize a combination studies, eyewitness reports (as well as interviews), photographs, and film footage of suspected quake-related lights, and have crafted several hypotheses behind their appearance. One published paper on the subject suggested that earthquake lights are possibly caused by the seismic stimulation of [the] inherent electrical properties of certain rocks under certain conditions.[26] Other theories for these strange lights include the proposal that they are the result of tectonic-induced

A photograph allegedly showing earthquake lights near Tagish Lake in the Canadian Yukon Territory, hours before the July, 1973 Cross Sound Earthquake. According to reports, the photo was taken by two boaters nearby on the lake.

disruptions of the Earth's magnetic field that prod quartz-bearing rocks to produce electrical charges when compressed in a certain way. Whatever their causes, the existence of earthquake lights adds to the speculation by geologists and other scientists that there are subtle (and not-so-subtle) environmental indicators of earthquakes that are present, but cannot be measured but our current level of technology and/or understanding.

---

[26] "Prevalence of Earthquake Lights Associated with Rift Environments." Seismological Research Letters, January/February 2014, v. 85, p. 159-178,

How to Prepare In The Event Of an Earthquake...

Understanding first that earthquakes tend to strike with virtually no warning, the best course(s) of action with regard to maintaining a degree of personal safety—property damage is given—is knowing what to do given the circumstances, and a quick response. This is essential since it's likely that individuals could potentially be anywhere or engaged in any type of activity when the ground underneath them begins shaking. As this may be the case, planning and/or responding to an earthquake should be made with the singular goal of protecting one's self from serious injury...or worse. And any response to an earthquake emergency should, like most natural disasters common to a particular area, be based on creating a prepared set of action plans.

Understand Your Earthquake Risk

Theoretically-speaking, earthquakes can potentially strike anywhere in the world. But the reality is that some areas around the globe are more earthquake-prone than others. The highest level of earthquake activity in the world occurs along the Pacific Rim's "ring of fire" (see page 22, and the map on page 23). In the U.S., the same reality holds true except that every state has experienced some level of seismic activity. This is to say that while every state has not experienced an actual earthquake in the strictest sense, every state *has* experienced either earthquakes or the seismic waves (i.e. shockwaves) from quakes that originated in nearby states...even from those states that rarely experience such seismic events. However, it is not as imperative that those residing in states like North and South Dakota be as prepared for the possibility of earthquakes as those residing on America's West Coast or those living near the New Madrid seismic zone.

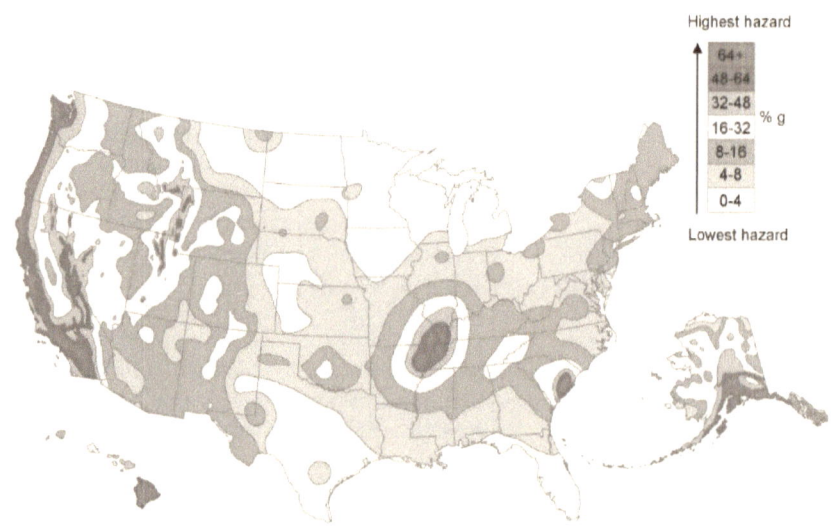

Highest hazard

64+
48-64
32-48
16-32   % g
8-16
4-8
0-4

Lowest hazard

Plan Your Actions.

Keeping in mind that earthquakes tend occur with virtually no warning, the foundation for any plan of action that should emphasize safety—regardless of where one might find themselves at the point an earthquake strikes. During a major earthquake, the possibility exists that most major services and/or utilities such as electricity, water, or landline phone service may be disrupted. Additionally, first responders—fire-rescue and the police—may be busy attending to other emergencies elsewhere (in most cases, first responders may be forced to either prioritize emergencies or arrive on-scene only as they are able to). In such an instance, there may be no immediate response to any call for assistance, so the ability to provide short-term self-sufficiency might become necessary. The best way to ensure that injuries, individual discomfort, and daily disruptions are minimized is to plan ahead. Suggested responses should entail the following actions:

Before An Earthquake
Create/Purchase an "Earthquake Emergency Kit

During a major earthquake, the possibility exists that most major services and/or utilities such as electricity, water, or landline phone service may be disrupted. Additionally, first responders—fire-rescue and the police—may be busy attending to other emergencies elsewhere (in most cases, first responders may be forced to either prioritize emergencies or arrive on-scene as they are able to). In such an instance, there may be no immediate response to any call for assistance, so the ability to provide short-term self-help might become necessary. The best way to ensure that food, water, minor medical, and information needs are met is to create (or purchase) an *earthquake emergency kit*.

In some instances, these kits can be purchased either online or in some brick-and-mortar stores (especially in earthquake-prone regions such as America's West Coast), prepackaged with most anticipated essentials. The prices of these prepackaged disaster kits will vary, depending on how stocked they are with supplies. Some pre-packaged kits contain basic supplies such as first aid kits, bottled water, and flashlights. The more expensive deluxe kits might include extra amenities such as a small portable toilet and/or water purification tablets in the event that the water supply is disrupted (a very distinct possibility given that waterlines and pipes tend to be underground).

However, effective disaster kits can just as easily be created by purchasing anticipated items individually, collecting and storing them in a designated location (such as a storage closet or detached shed). Once purchased or gathered together, emergency items should be stored in a container of some type, such as a moderate-sized plastic tote or foot locker capable of being sealed or closed for protection.

Depending on the potential earthquake hazard in a given location and the preparedness of an area's first-response infrastructure, a basic earthquake kit may be all that's required. However, there are instances in certain earthquake-prone regions where an earthquake occurs of such magnitude that basic services could be disrupted for several days. This was the case in the aftermath of the 1989 San Francisco earthquake, which resulted in the complete destruction of many homes that found many people with no immediate place left to go. In addition to the damage wrought by the earthquake itself, resulting fires added to the disruption of phone and other utility services. In such a case, a more extensive earthquake kit may be required to deal with the disruption of daily life and basic services for a period of anywhere between 72 hours to a week. At the very least, an effective disaster kit should include the following

An example of the type of plastic tote (with a sealed lid) which can be used to store an earthquake disaster kit. A footlocker of approximately the same size would be just as effective a storage location.

Clothing & Bedding:

- Several blankets, preferably one for every person in a family, or who for every individual who might be affected by a quake's aftermath. In addition to providing warmth, blankets can be folded into impromptu padded sleeping surfaces in the case of extended need (such as a dwelling becoming unstable and/or uninhabitable from earthquake damage). For the extra expense sleeping bags can be purchased in lieu of blankets, however, blankets are more practical and can be utilized for more multiple purposes in the event of an emergency (such as providing a measure of comfort to injured).

- Two pairs of sturdy work or safety gloves. Oftentimes, scattered debris and other structural pilings end up strewn across the immediate areas of structures damaged by earthquakes. In removing these obstructions, a sturdy pair of gloves would protect the hands from sharp edges and other potentially dangerous objects while moving trying to evacuate from or restore damaged structures.

Foodstuffs:

- Food is optional, but always a good idea. A 2-3 day supply of non-perishable, no refrigeration-required food should be packed away somewhere inside or near the shelter itself in the event of loss of power. Additionally, the foods selected for storage should be of the type that are tightly sealed, and requires very little or no preparation (i.e., cooking) and/or need for water. Ideally, food products with similarly close expiration dates should be purchased and stored together, so as to make replacing them at the same time easier if they expire before use.
  If storage space availability is limited, consider purchasing military-style Meals Ready to Eat (MRE) packet from surplus or camping stores. MREs are small packets of food rations that require just a little water or maybe some heat to prepare (but again, avoid the use of combustion sources of either heat and/or light in the event that gas leaks are discovered). Canned meats such as tuna and beef (jerky) have extended storage lives, so such items should be a main staple of any stored food (unless there are vegetarians present, in which case canned vegetables should be included).
- High energy food sources such as protein, energy, and/or granola bars are idea for storage. They require less space than canned foods, even those that don't require either preparation or refrigeration (which may not be available in the event that power is lost).
- Bottled water. In many cases, underground pipes and/or wells could be rendered non-functional during and after an earthquake. Stored in sealed plastic bottles, bottle water keeps amazingly well for extended periods. The U.S. Food and Drug Administration (FDA) estimates that most bottled water has a potentially indefinite shelf life, so replacing drinking water to maintain its availability in case of emergency use should not be a major concern. Ideally, one gallon of water per person, per day should be stored for emergencies. However, Nursing and/or pregnant women, children, and individuals with pre-existing medical conditions might need more water.
- Canned juices, milk, and/or soup (milk and soup can be purchased in powered form, and as such tend to have long shelf lives. Extra water should be considered if powdered foods are going to be used).
- Crackers, cookies, and other ready-to-eat snack foods add variety as well as supplement the food supply.

The No-Nonsense Guide To Earthquake Safety

Supplies/Communication:

- A source of light in the event of the loss of power. This preferably should not be flame-/fire-based sources of illumination due to the possibility (and likelihood) that gas pipes/lines might be damaged and/or exposed, creating an explosive hazard. The best source of light should be a rechargeable flashlight or penlight, or long-period glow sticks
- A battery-powered radio for keeping updated on vital information or instructions. A better alternative might be to consider purchasing one of the types of portable radios that rely on neither batteries nor electricity. These units are powered by cranking a handle, which charges a miniature generator inside the unit enough to power it *without* batteries or electricity for a limited amount of time.
- An all-purpose toolkit, or a multi-tool such as a heavy-duty Swiss army knife or Weatherman multi-purpose instrument. Tools and other such implements can be invaluable in the event that there is a need to clear debris and other obstructions from areas of protection and blocked evacuation paths leading from buildings and other structures.
- A non-electric/hand-powered can-opener (if not a function of a multi-purpose tool).
- A pack of batteries, preferably an assorted pack containing multiple sizes for battery-powered instruments (e.g., radio).
- Plastic utensils, paper plates, and/or Tupperware or plastic containers (with lids) for serving food.
- Sanitation supplies, in the event that any assistance is not immediate and facilities are not immediately available. A stock of sanitation supplies that includes toilet paper/towelettes, liquid bottled soap or detergent, a 5-gallon bucket with a lid, plastic garbage bags with ties, a disinfectant, a strong cleaner such as bleach, and personal hygiene items should be sufficient to lessen the hardships of extended periods without access to lavatory facilities (which may not be available is water pipers become ruptured during an earthquake).
- A first-aid kit. First-aid kits of varying degrees of items can be purchased at mostly any "big box" store, or can be created from scratch based on anticipated needs. At the very least, an effective first-aid kit should contain bandages (the plastic adhesive, rolled cloth, and/or the "liquid" varieties), roller cloth bandages, sterile gauze pads, towelette wipes, medical tape, a liquid antiseptic (e.g., alcohol and/or peroxide), anti-bacterial soap, smelling salts, petroleum jelly, latex gloves, tweezers, scissors, a thermometer, and aspirin or some other pain-reliever.
- A small, portable electric generator, in the event that electrical power is lost due to downed disrupted electrical services.
- A fire extinguisher (in the event of post-earthquake fires).

Earthquake Insurance

For those property-owners residing in earthquake-prone regions, it is worth considering purchasing earthquake insurance. While many homeowners/property owners and renters can purchase insurance policies that protect their homes and its contents against losses incurred from many forms of damage, most policies don't or won't automatically cover damage caused by natural disasters such as earthquakes or floods. For that reason, property owners should investigate the possibility of either specifically purchasing earthquake insurance coverage, or adding an earthquake endorsement[27] to existing insurance policies. In many instances, property owners' insurance and earthquake insurance coverage policies don't overlap. Instead, these co-policies work in tandem to protect property against many of the expected losses that may be incurred in an earthquake.

The decision as to whether one should purchase earthquake insurance depends on several factors, the primary one being how susceptible to earthquakes a particular geographical region is. As discussed previously, some seismically-active regions are more prone to earthquakes than others. While both Alaska and California are situated in high-activity earthquake zones, California's denser population and extensive infrastructures makes earthquake damage more of a probable likelihood than areas in less-populated Alaska.

A second factor is the likelihood of damage to a particular property in the event of an earthquake? Some dwellings, especially those in earthquake zones, are engineered to resist the worst of many average magnitude earthquakes. It may make far more financial sense to purchase full insurance coverage—including earthquake coverage—on an expensive home in an exclusive portion of a populated area than to attempt to purchase coverage on a cabin in a sparsely-populated region in the hinterlands.

Car Kit

✔ Canned food, manual can opener
✔ Nonperishable food:
instant nutrition bars, dried fruits, jerky, crackers, cookies

✔ Bottled water   ✔ Flashlight, batteries
✔ Extra clothing   ✔ Toilet tissue
✔ Sturdy shoes   ✔ Fire extinguisher
✔ Small first-aid kit   ✔ Street maps
✔ Blanket

Above: A sample emergency earthquake kit for automobiles

A final consideration with regard to purchasing earthquake insurance is the expected costs of rebuilding and/or recovering from an earthquake. Those considering earthquake coverage may need to consider relevant questions, such as how would living expenses (i.e., the cost of living) related to living elsewhere be covered while homes are being repaired—or rebuilt in worse-case scenarios? How much would still be owed to lenders/banks on the remaining (existing) amount (mortgage) still owed on a property—even though it might be destroyed as a result of a quake? And how much of a financial loss would be incurred on homes/properties that could not affordably be repaired? In the instance of some property owners, such as those who own valuable collectibles such as art, it might be necessary to purchase a separate policy to cover the value of the collectables. These are all valid concerns to consider when evaluating whether to purchase earthquake insurance beforehand.[28]

Other Pre-Earthquake Preparations

It is a good idea in earthquake-prone regions to not only have an emergency kit for the home, but a smaller version should be considered for personal vehicles as well. Additionally, there several other proactive courses of action that might help mitigate hazards and/or concerns during an earthquake.

---

[27] An endorsement is a written change to existing insurance policies that specifies under what/which conditions and circumstances property is to be protected against financial loss.

[28] See Appendix: G for a basic primer on what earthquake insurance is, what basic policies consist of, and what these policies cover.

The No-Nonsense Guide To Earthquake Safety

One option to consider is the purchase of a small metal lockbox, a safe, or some manner of highly resistant-to-damage container. The purpose of such an item is to store important papers and documents such as financial records, insurance papers, and birth certificates. Even without the threat of earthquake destroying a home, it's a good idea to keep such documents stored in damage-resistant container anyway to avoid their loss from other significant threats such as a house fire or a flood. A lockbox is also a secure place by which to keep another (possibly) anticipated necessity—money. Automatic Teller Machines (ATMs) may become disabled is power and computer networks become disrupted. Having emergency cash on-hand allows those who might be affected by a major earthquake to have a source of revenue in the event that temporary housing (e.g., motel) or food is needed.

It's also a good decision to minimize the various potential dangers and hazards around the home. One way to preempt potential hazards is to avoid placing heavy, large, and/or breakable objects on the highest level of a bookcase or shelf; such objects should be placed on lower shelves (the shelves themselves should also be secured). It's also a good decision to secure items like mirrors and pictures to walls (with strong adhesive made for just that purpose) away from couches, beds, and chairs—where people may sit and be struck if such items fell during an earthquake. Appliances and other household equipment such as water heaters, furnaces, and especially stoves should be secured by bolting them to the floor, or securing them to nearby walls. Additionally, flexible pipe fittings can limit the incidence of leaks. Overhead light fixtures and top-heavy objects should be braced and/or secured in a manner so as to prevent their falling or toppling in the event of violent shaking. Flammable and hazardous liquids should either be stored on lower-level shelving, or inside cabinets which can be fastened (or locked) securely. In earthquake-frequent regions such as California, other options are usually available to homeowners in order to help mitigate earthquake hazards.[29]

Finally, whether the situation concerns a home, business, school, or other type of institution, drills—or at the very least reviews—that reinforce contingency plans should be undertaken at regular intervals. Many public schools (as well as private and government employers) in Japan, California, and other seismically-active regions have regular earthquake drills that instill the appropriate response of taking cover when earthquake tremors begin (see: page 41). What's more, if there are several assigned emergency roles for individuals in the event of an earthquake drill, these individuals should be routinely reminded of their responsibilities for as long as they are assigned said responsibility. For example, one person might be responsible for disconnecting utilities such as gas, electricity, and/or water that might pose serious and/or potentially lethal hazards should, say gas lines rupture.[30] That individual would need to not only know where the instruments (i.e., tools) are located to shut off any affected utility/utilities, but also know how to use them effectively.

---

[29] One example of these additional precautions available homeowners in earthquake-prone regions is the addition of automatic shut-off valves to gas-based furnaces. These devices, when installed can immediately terminate the flow of gas to furnaces whenever seismic vibrations are present—lessening the probability of both gas leaks and/or fires. In addition, California residents can seek out licensed building contractors who provide consultation, suggestions, and price quotes for potential seismic-related preparation for property-owners (such as securing furnaces, refrigerators, and other heavy objects that may present a potential hazard during a quake).

[30] In the event that the gas utility needs to be shut off in the aftermath of an earthquake (or earthquake drill), DO NOT try to relight the gas pilot flame. This can cause the gas to leak and cause a fire. Call the utility company or building maintenance and have them do it instead.

During An Earthquake

Seeking Protection

When an earthquake begins, there may only be a few moments to realize what is happening. Despite the surprise factor of such an event, the first reaction is to stay calm, and avoid the urge to panic! Wherever someone may be during an earthquake, the primary goal should be to **protect themselves from potential harm!** And being aware of one's surroundings provides a basis for thinking about how to best to protect one's self… whether it be at home, work, while driving, or in a public location. In each case, experts in the fields of medicine, public safety, earthquake research, as well as advisors within the insurance industry have offered suggestions as to the best courses of action(s) to take in many potential earthquake-related situations.

Indoors (Homes & Single Story Buildings)

If indoors when an earthquake occurs, the best course of action is to remain indoors and resist the urge to either evacuate the building or run into other rooms. Instead of standing and trying to keep from falling, the chances of injury can be reduced by practicing a version of "duck and cover." This suggested course of action entails a three-part response:

- The first of these responses is to *drop to a position on the hands and knees* when the tremors begin. Doing so prevents being knocked off balance by the shaking of the ground during the quake, but still allows movement related to the second part of the response.
- *Covering the head and neck* (and/or the entire body, if possible). The best way to ensure that these vulnerable parts of the body are "covered" is to take cover underneath a sturdy table or desk (many children attending public schools in high-earthquake frequent regions are drilled in this technique by doing so under their desks). Crawling quickly on the hands and knees helps maintain the body's balance during the shaking, while still allowing for the ability to seek cover quickly. But in the event that there are no furnishings available to use as cover, ducking and covering should take place next to an interior wall (avoid taking cover next to exterior walls/walls adjacent to the outside of a structure). Another option in the absence of a table or desk is next to crouch and cover near a low-lying piece of furniture that's stable enough not to fall during the shaking.   Any such covering/shelter should be taken—if possible—away from dangling objects (e.g., ceiling fixtures), top-heavy objects or furniture, or fireplaces that could tip over. Kitchens are a particularly dangerous room to seek shelter in because of the presence of heavy appliances and loose objects such as utensils.[31]
- *Hold on.* Wherever or whatever object that is used to take cover under, hold on to the object (or in the case where no object and/or furniture is available, hold on to the head and neck) until

---

[31] Additionally, the possibility of broken and damaged pipes further makes kitchens a dangerous place to seek shelter during an earthquake. Gas pipes create an immediate danger, such as a gas leak and resulting explosion, if leaking gas comes into contact with an open flame or other ignition source. In the event that an individual finds themselves in a kitchen during an earthquake, the best course of action should be to either quickly turn off any gas-powered stove/oven or the gas line itself (most gas lines have shut-off valves at the connection point), and take cover at the first sign of shaking, or (if possible) avoid taking shelter in the kitchen altogether.

the shaking ends. In some rare cases, it may be necessary to move with the improvised shelter if the ground begins to shift around.

In addition to taking cover, there are actions which one can do to reduce the likelihood of injury. If indoors during an earthquake, within the first few moments of the quake—before the shaking intensifies, quickly move away from windows, which will likely produce shattering glass with sharp edges as a cutting hazard. Additionally, attempt to move away from unsecured furnishings such as bookcases and/or china cabinets that can become crushing and/or falling hazards during a quake. Lastly, be aware of falling objects such as bricks from fireplaces and chimneys, over-hanging light fixtures (e.g., ceiling fans and the like), wall hangings, pictures, and loose objects that may be found on secured (or unsecured) shelving.

Nighttime and early-morning quakes are particularly dangerous because of the high likelihood that many people will be sleep, and suddenly being startled awake by the ground shaking could cause immediate panic. According to several medical and scientific analyses of earthquake injuries, many individuals who attempted to get out of bed during a quake were injured by doing so. In the majority of cases, the injuries could have easily been prevented if individuals had remained in bed instead. In the event that anyone finds themselves in a similar situation, there are actually two recommended options. The first course of action is to remain put; stay in the bed and cover the head with a pillow. The second option is to roll out of the bed and quickly roll underneath. The combination of the bed's box spring and mattress should provide protection against falling objects. Since being struck by falling objects and airborne projectiles is the greatest single cause of injuries suffered during an earthquake, being aware of loose and vulnerable objects prior to—and avoiding their impact during—a quake is the surest way to avoid becoming an earthquake casualty.

Indoors (Multi-story & High Rise Buildings)

For those who might find themselves in multi-story dwellings during an earthquake, the suggested course of action is fairly much the same as a single-floor dwelling; drop to hands and knees, get to cover, and hold to wherever cover is sought. If such a building is a crowded public venue, the urge to panic and/or rush for the exits should be avoided as well. The safest recourse is to simply maintain a low position (near the floor) and protect the head and neck with the arms and hands and neck with your hands and arms. However, there are some other concerns to consider in seeking cover in multi-story buildings. Perhaps the biggest of these concerns is the belief that taller buildings are likely to collapse in an earthquake.

The truth is that a building collapse is far from a certainty based on several relevant variables involved. One of these variables lies in the construction of the buildings in seismically-active regions. In developed countries such as the U.S., New Zealand, and Japan, local and regional ordinances require structures erected in seismically-active regions adhere to strict *building codes*.[32] These codes mandate that newer houses, buildings, and other-related structures be engineered and constructed in a way as to make them resistant to the effects of ground shaking due to seismic-related events (see page 20). In areas of the world there is very little in the way of building codes—especially those related to resisting earthquake tremors—structural collapse tends to occur far more often during a major earthquake. By comparison in the U.S., Japan, and other advanced countries with earthquake-prone areas, the overwhelming majority of buildings do not collapse at all...with total collapses being a rare event indeed.

As a result of earthquake-related building codes, taller buildings in earthquake zones are designed to sway back and forth rather than break. This is to say multi-storied buildings that have been earthquake-engineered will not readily collapse, unless the magnitude of a particular earthquake exceeds their tolerance levels.[33] And because of these stringent standards that make a building collapse unlikely (although not a 0% unlikelihood), those forced to take cover in multi-story buildings are just as likely to survive an earthquake by ducking and covering in the same way as they would in a single-story dwelling. This should take place either under a sturdy object or against an interior wall in the building away from windows (otherwise the combination of broken windows and the building's sway could cause individuals to be ejected from the building). Once the earthquake stops, inhabitants should exit the building, avoiding the use of elevators and instead use stairways.

But in the rare event—at least in the industrialized world—that a building collapses occurs during the course of an earthquake, a person is statistically *more* likely to survive such an ordeal taking advantage of cover than attempting to run out of a shaking building. Rescue and first-responders are trained to search collapsed structures in a way as to be capable of identifying potential gaps and spaces where survivors might be located in these circumstances.

Another factor that determines whether a building can resist structural collapse during an earthquake is the duration of the quake itself. Every earthquake is different in terms of their hypocenters/epicenters, each quake's point of focus from population centers, where in the quake occurs, and their overall effects. This means that each individual earthquake will vary in terms of how long or their effects will last over a particular area. The logical implication with regard to the structural of buildings is that most buildings in developed areas can weather most light, moderate, and even major earthquakes fairly well given the average duration of past quakes—under a minute long.

Outdoors

---

[32] See Appendix: F for supplemental information on building codes related to the history earthquake engineering.

[33] Examples of factors accompanying earthquakes that could conceivably increase the likelihood of collapse in an earthquake-engineered building include quakes of a prolonged duration (earthquakes longer than 60 seconds), and quakes with an epicenter very close to a building's location.

Again, since earthquakes tend to happen with very little warning, it's possible that an individual can be virtually anywhere when one *does* occur. In the event that anyone should find themselves outside when an earthquake starts, its best to either get to or stay out in the open. While out in the open, it is advisable to stay clear of street lamps, utility poles, buildings, power lines and anything else that could potentially fall on those nearby. Once out in the open, those seeking to avoid earthquake-related injury should remain sheltered in place by getting low to the ground until the shaking stops. This is considered the most effective course of action simply because [the] ground movement during an earthquake is rarely ever the direct cause of death or injury. Most earthquake-related casualties result from collapsing walls, flying glass, and falling objects.

In mountainous and/or hilly regions, people should be aware of the potential for avalanches and seismically-induced landslides (see page 14). Depending on the stability of the ground in these regions, landslides triggered by earthquakes can begin at the time of the shaking or in the immediate aftermath of a quake. And even if the rocks and the other earthen material that make up landslides and avalanches holds through the initial earthquake, they may become loose enough over a period of time after the quake to remain a hazard for up to a few months afterwards.

Those residing in earthquake zones near an ocean or sea have to be especially cautious in the aftermath of an earthquake. Earthquakes with an area of focus either within regions near a coast or offshore—even those hundreds of miles/kilometers in the middle of the ocean—may trigger a destructive and potentially deadly tsunami (see page 15). People living in these areas should assume that a tsunami is likely after a quake, and immediately evacuate to higher ground to avoid the drowning hazard that may follow should nearby ocean waters begin moving inward.

Public Venues

The recommended responses to an occurring earthquake will differ from venue to venue. This is because the potential hazards for each area or location will vary because of factors like building design, the presence and scope of nearby municipal infrastructure, local geology, etc. Additionally, the very purpose of a public venue lends another level either mitigating or exacerbating potential dangers in an earthquake.

For example, a crowded supermarket or store may have loaded shelves stacked high enough to cause serious injury or even death should they tumble on an unsuspecting victim during a quake. What's more, the often busy environment of stores suddenly interrupted by an earthquake can change the atmosphere from one of order and relative calm to one chaos and general panic. And as a point of fact, panic in itself can have rash consequences leading to injuries and/or even death. For anyone who finds themselves in a public setting such as a store during an earthquake, the first recommended course of action should be to move away from unsecured objects and/or structures that might topple during the shaking. This means that individuals should immediately move away from shelves, display cases, or other similar furnishings. A general rush for the exit(s) should also be avoided, as many others will no-doubt attempt to flee the building at the same time.

The same advice is recommended in other places of public accommodation, such as movie theaters and open arena/stadiums. The first recommended response is to stay calm and quickly consider the options for places to seek cover. In many cases, the best alternative among the few existing options is to duck and cover under the seating, while covering the head and neck with the hands and arms. The same course of actions should be followed if an earthquake occurs in an open stadium. These public areas should be evacuated only when the ground stops quaking, and in a calm orderly manner.

In a Subway

Like skyscrapers, many people fear that subways risk collapse during an earthquake. The truth is, most modern underground transportation systems, especially those in earthquake-prone areas have been engineered to resist seismic activity (much like many tall buildings in those regions). In fact, there has never been a single documented case on record of a subway collapse due to earthquakes. What's

Affect of Seismic Activity on Subway Tunnels

Earthquake	Date	Magnitude	Impact on Subway
Mexico City	1985	8.1	No damage to tunnels. Some power disruption. Patrons evacuated safely. Used to transport rescue personnel.
Loma Prieta (SF)	1989	6.9	No damage to tunnels. Subway served as lifeline structure.
Northridge	1994	6.7	No damage
Kobe, Japan	1995	7.2	No damage to tunnels. Damage to station and sewer pipes – attributed to 1962 design with moderate seismic provision
Taipei	2002	6.8	No damage
Chile	2010	8.8	Running next day. Some damage at entrance to stations

more, some subway systems such as those in Japan and California are equipped with electronic auto shut-down features than bring all subway train traffic in the tunnels to an immediate halt if significant ground-shaking is detected. Such safety features make responding to an earthquake inside subways as relatively unproblematic as doing so within any other structure.

If an earthquake occurs while in a subway, the preferred course of action is the same as in most other venues. Occupants of a subway experiencing an earthquake should drop to the floor/ground, cover their heads and necks, and hold on either under subway seating, or next to them until the earthquake stops. If those inside the subway are on an adjoining waiting platform rather than on the train itself, cover should be sought under any nearby bench/seating.

There is a possibility that once an earthquake stops, electrical power to the subway may be interrupted. In this event, it may become necessary to manually open subway car doors. Once this is done successfully, everyone should exit both the train and the subway itself in an orderly fashion.

While Driving

In the aftermath of the 1989 San Francisco (*Loma Prieta*) Earthquake, news footage was aired around the world showing people's reactions to the quake as it occurred. Among the most noted of those images were those related to drivers who found themselves suddenly impacted by the quake as they drove home from work (the quake struck around 5pm local time, the so-called "rush hour" of heavy traffic). Dozens of automobiles were heavily damaged or destroyed, and their drivers injured—with several killed—as they panicked and failed to take actions that would have lessened their chances of becoming casualties.

Drivers who suddenly find themselves faced with attempting to navigate on quaking ground should slow down and attempt to drive their vehicles out of traffic as soon as the shaking begins.[34] Drivers

Many drivers were caught unprepared during the sudden onset of the 1989 San Francisco Earthquake, many of them while driving on the areas bridges.

should then stop and park their vehicles out of the flow of traffic until the shaking stops. Parking on bridges and overpasses/underpasses should be avoided. Drivers should also steer clear of parking near trees, utility/light poles, power lines, and other height-based objects that could potentially .

Once the ground shaking subsides, drivers should resume driving—getting out of a vehicle should only done as necessary. Roads and streets may contain debris and other hazards (such as live power lines) as a result of the quake, so drivers should be vigilant of these potential issues. Drivers should also be

---

[34] Most times in all but the most powerful magnitude earthquakes, it is often difficult to perceive that an earthquake is occurring to those driving. Many drivers have reported the only indication that they had of an earthquake even occurring while driving was a feeling that it felt "like there is something wrong with (their) car, such as a flat tire." This lack of awareness was seen in video footage from the 1989 San Francisco Earthquake as several drivers were seen traveling unawares toward large gaps in the nearby Oakland Bay Bridge, created as large sections of the bridge collapsed during the near 7.0 magnitude quake.

aware of the presence of emergency vehicles heading towards or parking where emergency services are needed, so these vehicles should be given the right-of-way. It is also advisable that drivers should also tune their radios to local stations for reports of damaged roads, bridges, and other driving routes. The use of phones, except in actual emergencies should be avoided after a major earthquake, as the lines will undoubtedly be tied up with similar calls for assistance (if possible, consider texting for assistance, as texting—not advisable while driving—doesn't tie up phone lines as much).

After An Earthquake

Immediate Aftermath

Depending on the magnitude as well as the extent of damage incurred as the result of a particular earthquake, the recovery time for both affected individuals and communities can vary anywhere from hours to months...or even years. In every case, individuals impacted by an earthquake will need to assess the extent of this impact as well as diminish any present hazards resulting from the event. Ideally, the earliest response should begin the moment an individual steps out of cover.

The first action after the shaking stops is to ensure that it's actually safe to move. After coming from under cover, individuals should check both themselves and others for any potential injuries. Assuming that no one is trapped under any wreckage or rubble, those with access to emergency supplies—ideally with access to a complete emergency earthquake kit (see pages 37-38)—should utilize first aid materials to treat any injuries. Those with more serious injuries should not be moved, unless there are immediate hazards nearby (such as a fire) which could make those injuries worse. Serious and/or critical injuries may also require an emergency call to 9-1-1 emergency assistance. However, those in critical need should be aware that phone lines—both cellular and landlines—may be busy due to the possibility of many other calls for assistance.

If there are no serious injuries, it may be prudent to begin inspecting the premises for major damage; this is especially true for property owners. All pipes and wiring—gas, water, and electrical—should be inspected for damage. If hazardous damages and/or leaks are detected (such as sparking electrical wires or damaged gas lines smelling of gas), valves and/or power supplies should be shut off. If the smell of leaking gas is noticeable after an earthquake, windows and doors should be opened to help dissipate the fumes and the premises evacuated immediately. **Do not use an ignition source such as a lighter, matches, or candles to look for damaged pipes** (as this could result in an explosion or fire if gas is present)! Instead, use either a glow stick or a flashlight to inspect for such damage. After any repairs, gas service should be restored only by a licensed professional.

In inspecting for electrical-related issues, the smell of burning insulation and the sight of broken or frayed wires (especially if accompanied by sparks) are indications of electrical damage. If any of these indicators are present after an earthquake (or other natural disaster), it is advisable to disconnect the electrical service from the fuse box and/or circuit breaker. Stepping in any standing water (due to the possibility of broken or damaged pipes) in order to disconnect electrical service is extremely dangerous, and should be avoided! In such a circumstance, contact a professional electrician.

And on the subject of water, water pipes and sewage lines should likewise be inspected for damage. Damage to plumbing systems can impede with both water supplies as well as interfere with sanitation, a potential long-term health hazard in itself. If damage to the water and/or plumbing systems is noted, the use of toilets should be stopped, and drinking water from the tap should be avoided until it is deemed safe to resume use (the local or regional water utilities authority should be contacted with regard to such issues). Safe drinking water from a prepared emergency kit can be used until these services are restored. In worse-case scenarios, safe water can be obtained from undamaged water heaters or by melting ice cubes.

If electrical power hasn't been disrupted, tuning in to local television and/or radio news is recommended. In severe quakes, local authorities will likely be issuing important information and/or instructions via the news media. In the event that electrical power isn't available, a battery-operated or crank-powered radio (or television) should be accessible, especially in high-earthquake probability zones where the need could easily arise. Additionally, most newer-model cell phones have internet browsing capabilities that allow users to have at least some access to emergency information or instructions on news and/or government websites.

Depending on the immediate post-earthquake circumstances and extent of the damage, a higher priority might be placed on a search for fires or areas of obvious smoldering material. If small fires are observed starting up, they should be extinguished immediately using available resources. Doing so will prevent small fires from spreading and becoming a major after-earthquake hazard.[35] Fires in the aftermath of the 1906 San Francisco earthquake raged for 3 days, resulting in an even greater level of damage than that created by the earthquake itself.

Lastly, another potential hazard to be aware of is the possibility of aftershocks. Aftershocks, particularly likely after a moderate or powerful earthquake, can vary in intensity themselves. In fact, aftershocks can occur at intensities large enough to cause additional or new damage in their own right. The anticipation of aftershocks should be a part of post-earthquake measures, as they can interfere with repair and recovery process. And since aftershocks can occur in the first few hours, days, or even weeks after a major quake, the same contingency planning used in anticipation of earthquakes should be in place for aftershock. The strategy of dropping, covering, & holding is the best response to aftershocks.

In coastal regions and on islands, inhabitants should be aware of the increased chances for the occurrence of a tsunami—or of a seiche[36] (pronounced saysh) near large inland bodies of water. Considered "seismic sea waves," these earthquake-triggered hazards can quickly raise the water levels

---

[35] Fires in fact are the single most common hazard following earthquakes.

[36] A seiche is a large-scale sloshing of water in a back and forth motion similar to that that occurs in a bathtub or sink. A phenomenon that occurs within semi-or fully-enclosed bodies of water, seiches have two main causes. The first cause stems from intense weather conditions that cause rapid changes in atmospheric pressure. The second, more relevant major cause is earthquakes. Seiche conditions tend push water from one end of an enclosed body of water to the other, causing it oscillate back and forth for hours or even days after the initiating event. Although seiches are not as common as tsunamis, this particular instability of inland water can cause damage to nearby property by way of flooding and water damage to nearby structures.

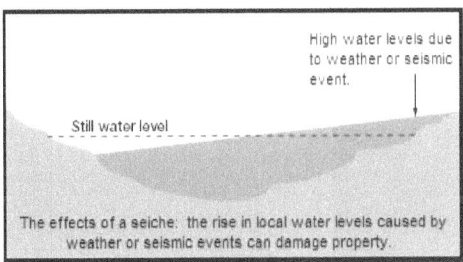

The effects of a seiche: the rise in local water levels caused by weather or seismic events can damage property.

along adjacent lands that can cause immediate flooding and tidal-like surges that can sweep away both property and lives in a matter of moments—with very little warning. If or when local authorities issue a tsunami warning after an earthquake, it is best to assume that a series of potentially dangerous tidal surges are imminent. Beaches and waterfronts of all kinds should be avoided after an earthquake.

Although not obvious, others may be in need of assistance. If there are no immediate problems arising from damage or personal safety, it is always a good idea to check on the wellbeing of neighbors. Those with large families may need additional assistance in emergency situations. Also, the elderly and individuals with disabilities may require additional assistance.

Intermediate Aftermath

After the most pressing concerns—curtailing any hazards arising from an earthquake—are addressed, attention should turn toward recovery in the intermediate timeframe afterwards. This level of recovery should emphasize aspects of assessing the extent of resources needed to regain a sense of pre-quake normalcy for those affected. This level may also include some level of reducing other potential hazards—those not immediately apparent—in the long-term sense.

One aspect of the intermediate recovery phase that exhibits both, the potential assessment of needs for recovery and hazard mitigation is the need to inspect property that might have been damaged in the earthquake. Building damage stemming from earthquakes can often occur where it's least expected...or found right away. For this reason, it might be prudent to invite professionals building inspectors to inspect earthquake-impacted properties, especially as they relate to older buildings that might have been built prior to modern building codes and earthquake-resistant engineering.

A thorough inspection might reveal damage in places and at points within structures that might be easily missed by either a superficial examination or one performed by less-experienced individuals. Unnoticed damage could lead to future hazards that may not manifest themselves for some time after an earthquake. For example, unnoticed cracks in chimneys caused by a recent earthquake can be the cause of a fire years after the quake

To help facilitate inspections, it may be a good idea for everyone to leave the premises until it is deemed safe to enter (if a building has experienced obvious or noticeable damage, said building should be evacuated immediately before aftershocks occur). All walls, floor, doors, staircases, and windows should be examined to ensure that there are no damages, and that the building is structurally sound. It is especially important to check the roof as well as the foundation of a dwelling for damages that could lead to critical damage of the entire structure.[37] As in the case of the immediate aftermath of an earthquake, battery-powered lanterns or flashlights should be used to inspect buildings and homes, as kerosene lanterns, candles, and matches may tip over or ignite any nearby flammables (it is also wise to avoid smoking inside, as this too could trigger a fire).

At this point, it is an excellent idea to take pictures of any damage, of both damaged contents and actual structural damage. Pictures will help expedite any monetary insurance claims that might be filed to cover the cost of rebuilding damaged buildings as well as replace lost property. Additionally, a

---

[37] In the event that homes and/or apartment dwellings are damaged beyond the point where they can be safely inhabited, it will become necessary to secure temporary shelter until such time that long-term housing can be obtained. In such an instance, it might be necessary to evacuate to a designated public shelter. In the U.S., residents in earthquake disaster zones have the option of using their cell phones to locate such shelters by texting SHELTER + your ZIP code to 43362 (4FEMA) to find the nearest shelter in the nearest area (example: shelter 12345). If it becomes necessary for individuals to actually leave their homes, emergency supplies /emergency kits (as well as other essentials) should be taken along. When vacating a property, it's a good policy to post a message in clear view of others indicating the point of relocation.

prepared list (and/or photographs) of the more expensive items within a home/building will aid in expediting any potential insurance claims for damage coverage.[38]

Any spilled liquids, especially those that could be hazardous to personal health or the environment should be cleaned up as soon as it's feasible to do so. Spilled medicines, cleaning products (e.g., bleach), or flammable liquids (e.g., gasoline) could create a chemical emergency, and possibly contaminate water and/or sewage systems if left uncontained. Also, closet and cabinet doors should be opened cautiously. Any liquid or solid contents may have shifted during the shaking of an earthquake and could fall (or spill) should they be uncontained suddenly (and creating the potential for further damage and/or injury).

For those seeking to recoup financial losses incurred during an earthquake, an inventory of items and/or property loss should be taken. Insurers should be contacted, and a prepared list of the most expensive and/or crucial items lost should be given to insurance adjusters or agents (having a prepared list of vulnerable possessions is more of a preparation imperative in earthquake-prone regions than in areas where earthquakes are relatively rare). In some cases, it might be prudent to take photographs or even video of vulnerable or particularly valuable assets beforehand to demonstrate losses. If possible, be prepared to show receipts for expensive items purchased (with the caveat that insurance companies cover the estimated value of losses, not the purchase costs of items).

Finally, the emotional well-being of children (and adults) should be monitored. Intense experiences such as natural disasters can have an adverse affect on an individual's sense of security. In worse-case scenarios, those who have experienced the negative effects of a major earthquake may require counseling or therapy in order to help them cope. Both children' and adults' sense of security may need to be reinforced with the help of professional mental health assistance, particularly if the experience was intense enough to produce behavioral changes that warrant intervention

Likewise, animal behavior—especially pets—should be observed closely after an earthquake. Often after a major natural disaster, the behavior of pets may change dramatically. Normally quiet dogs and friendly cats may become more defensive, even aggressive after an earthquake. If such changes in pet behavior becomes noticeable, pet dogs should be leashed (if possible) and place them in an enclosed area such as a fenced yard. At any rate, pets should be comforted after a natural disaster. If evacuation becomes necessary, pets should be taken to a pre-identified pet-friendly shelter.

---

[38] Note: In nearly every instance, insurance payouts for covered items or contents will be calculated in a way as to cover the cost of replacing a lost or damage item, and not necessarily the actual cost paid for an item at the time of purchase. It is for this reason that it is recommended that property owners to have a list of valuable contents. Policy holders may want to verify this point with their insurers of record.

What to Avoid

As there are in most predictable natural disasters like hurricanes and tornadoes, there are common-sense rules one should observe when confronted with an unpredictable event like an earthquake. These rules entail avoiding actions that could increase the likelihood for injury or death, while adhering to practices and precautions that could help ensure escaping injury (or death). And as more and more research reveals a greater understanding of earthquakes and their damaging effects, what we once thought and/or believed to have been the best possible courses of actions to keep safe during a quake have been reevaluated. Moreover, while it's a near-certainty that many life-or-death decisions made by individuals during an earthquake might be made based on individual and distinct circumstances, many general practices meant to lessen the probability of injury (or death) still apply for nearly every earthquake—individual circumstances notwithstanding.

Many of these potentially life-saving decisions are based on actions and decisions we should avoid taking. These actions include:

- Standing in a doorway. This now-outdated custom once practiced by those living in earthquake-prone regions has been debunked given the abundance of new data regarding earthquake safety. It is highly advised that individuals **DO NOT stand in a doorway** during an earthquake. In analyzing the structures of most modern homes, research indicates that doorways are no stronger than any other part of the house.[39] In fact, taking cover in doorways will invariably fail to protect individuals from the most probable source of earthquake injuries and deaths–falling or flying objects (e.g., small television sets, lamps, glass objects, bookcases, etc.).
- **DO NOT run outside or to other rooms during an earthquake.** Research suggests that immediately taking cover under a sturdy object such as a table—as opposed to attempting to exit a building—is far less likely to result in injury to those seeking to run outside. Additionally, the area near the exterior walls of a building is the most dangerous location in terms of where *not* to be during an earthquake. Windows, facades and architectural details are often the first parts of the building to collapse. To stay away from this danger zone, stay inside if you are inside and outside if you are outside. Also, shaking can be so strong that you will not be able to move far without falling down, and objects may fall or be thrown at you that you do not expect. Injuries can be avoided if you drop to the ground before the earthquake drops you.
- Using the "Triangle of Life" strategy during an earthquake. This strategy involves sheltering near a solid item as opposed to ducking and covering. The theory holds that crouching right next to a solid object such as a couch, bed, or heavy shelving will provide a protective space in which a person might be able survival should the dwelling collapses around them. However, this theory is based on the expectation that debris is likely to fall in a certain way during an earthquake.

---

[39] While it is true that that in most modern homes/buildings, doorways are no stronger than other parts of that dwelling, this is not necessarily true of older homes. In older wood frame homes and/or those constructed of adobe, interior doorways tended to have been built sturdier, partly to support the weight of nearby walls. Before relatively recent research to the contrary, it is this fact that gave initial credence to the belief that standing in a doorway during an earthquake was the best course of action one can take to reduce risk of injury or death. However, ducking and taking cover under a heavy and/or sturdy object such as a table is the best decision.

This is to say that it very difficult to know where these supposed "protective spaces" will be formed, as objects (including large, heavy objects) often move around during earthquakes.

The theoretical principle behind the "triangle of life" strategy some argue will ensure survival during an earthquake in the event of a structure's collapse.

However, statistical studies of earthquake deaths indicate that most injuries and deaths occur due to falling objects, not structures. Also, since it is nearly impossible to predict the exact manner in which walls and/or debris will fall (or shift) during an earthquake anyway, *many experts do not advise using the triangle strategy.* Stick to the duck and cover plan of action.

- Do not attempt to drive during an earthquake (see pages 45-46).
- Exploring (or sight-seeing around) damaged areas. Unless there is either a general call for assistance or if one has a particular area of needed expertise (such as a doctor, nurse, or other vocation), damaged areas should be avoided by everyone except for personnel affiliated with law enforcement, fire-rescue, or relief organizations. Likewise, severely-damaged buildings should never be entered; unless there are extenuating circumstances such as providing assistance—*and only if* there is no risk of self-harm.

Earthquake Myths

Over the years, many myths regarding earthquakes have taken root among our general beliefs. Although it is a safe to assume that no one (still) believes that earthquakes are the result of angry deities or curses, there are still many other erroneous myths that continue to resist all efforts to put them to rest. Some of these myths are based on a tradition of beliefs, while others are predicated on false assumptions made on superficial observations about past earthquakes. Still others are the result of movie producers taking liberties with the laws of physics and overly-dramatic special effects.

Whatever their origins, accepting earthquake myths can cause more potential harm than not for the believer. Individual decisions made in the midst of an earthquake based on these myths can conceivably end in harm, even death. In order better make informed decisions about earthquake safety, it is necessary to separate earthquake myths from facts, as supported by empirical data, a general consensus of the scientific community, and other noted experts on earthquake safety. Among the generally-held earthquake myths that continue to propagate are:

- During an earth, the ground can "open up" and "swallow people."

Contrary to the belief, this simply does not occur during earthquakes. While it's true that open fissures may form in the ground (large enough for an adult human to fit within) during an earthquake, the ground does not spontaneously open up beneath an individual's feet whereby they can fall into. This myth is mostly the result of the imaginations of motion picture producers.

- Animals can "predict" earthquakes.

The most realistic response to this general belief is not per se. However, there are hundreds of documented cases where animal behavior has been observed to have noticeably—drastically so in some cases—changed prior to the occurrence of an earthquake. The sheer number of these cases has prompted scientists to examine whether there is a link between earthquakes and changes in animal behavior. While there have been some noticeable scientific correlations between the two events— particularly in some particular animal species—changes in animal behavior before an earthquake are generally not consistent enough to prove a tangible link. While it is advised that any widespread noticeable changes in animal behavior in and/or near earthquake-prone regions should be given a level of greater attention, such changes should not be taken as a confirmation of an impending seismic event.

- A major earthquake will cause the state of California could fall into the Pacific Ocean.

According to seismologists and other experts on plate tectonics, this is simply not a conceivable event. This is because the2 major tectonic plates that comprise the famed San Andreas Fault System do not act in a manner consistent with such a scenario. The Pacific Plate tends to movie in one direction, while the

North American plate in another—opposite to the direction needed for the state actually to sink into the ocean.

- Small earthquakes prevent larger earthquakes.

Not necessarily true. In many cases, smaller earthquakes—even a large a cluster—cannot generate the total level of energy equal to the amount released in a single larger earthquake. So while smaller quakes may ease the pent-up tectonic stresses on a fault line temporarily, they do not produce the potential seismic energy to prevent larger quakes.

- People can cause earthquakes.

Generally this is a myth, but to an extent. While it is true that human beings cannot cause earthquakes on demand, there are cases where human activity has been known (or suspected) to have triggered a level of seismic activity (e.g., extracting fossil fuels, see page 8 for an example of this). Earthquakes caused by such activity tend to be of a minor magnitude. However, other related activity such as deep mining can actually cause moderate-magnitude quakes. But generally-speaking, human activities have not been shown to trigger earthquakes.

Summary

   Although our knowledge and understanding of earthquakes has increased over the centuries, our relative vulnerability to these geological-based natural disasters has not. We are just as likely to be injured or killed in any given risk-manner—being struck by falling objects, crushed by toppling heavy furnishings or structural collapse, or killed by aftermath effects such as fires—resulting from earthquakes today as we might have been in times past.   And while it is true that our increased understanding of earthquake science has lead to crafting ways to make ourselves *less* vulnerable (e.g., earthquake resistant buildings, seismic wave detection systems, and a basic understanding of physics), such understanding still doesn't protect us from experiencing the potential damage, death, and destruction a major earthquake can bring.

   However, individuals, families, and vulnerable communities can and *should* take the initiative and become responsible for their own safety. Contingency plans for those who reside in an area frequented by certain natural disasters such as earthquakes should be made *before* a predictable crisis. It can literally make the difference between life and death in knowing which decisions to make about the safest places to take shelter prior to the need.   Since it is statistically more likely that an earthquake will strike particular areas of both a country and the world on the whole, being prepared for the possibility will increase the chances that an individual will escape the experience relatively safe should it happen.

Notes

Earthquake History

The following earthquakes provide an illustration of the varying impact and effects of these seismic events on localized and expanded areas in and around where they occur.

Date	Location	Impact/Significance
January 23, 1556	Shaanxi Province, China	Considered not only the deadliest earthquake in history, but also the deadliest natural disaster in recorded human history. With an estimated magnitude of between 8.0 and 8.3, the earthquake resulted in the deaths of an estimated 833,000 thousand people. Most of those who perished were crushed to death as shallow caves (where many made their homes) and poorly-constructed dwellings collapsed on top of them.
May 22, 1960	Around Valdivia and Concepción, Chile	The most powerful earthquake ever recorded. Measuring an astounding 9.5 on the Richter scale, this quake killed between 3,000 and 6,000 people in Chile, Hawaii (in the U.S.), Japan, and the Philippines. Most of those deaths stemmed from a combination of result of the quake itself, a tsunami in the Pacific Ocean region adjacent to the quake's epicenter, landslides, and flooding in affected areas of Chile.
March 27, 1964	Southern-central area of Alaska	The Good Friday earthquake of 1964 was the most powerful earthquake in American history, and the 2nd most powerful earthquake ever recorded. Lasting over 4 and a half minutes duration, the magnitude 9.2 quake created an area of damage that stretched into areas of the American Northwest region.
December 26, 2004	Underneath the Indian Ocean, near Sumatra, Indonesia	A day after Christmas, 2004, a powerful magnitude 9.3 earthquake occurred under the Indian Ocean near the coast of the island nation

		of Indonesia. The 3rd most powerful earthquake ever recorded, the quake triggered a massive tsunami that affected areas of Indonesia, Sri Lanka, India, Thailand, the Maldives, and the coast of Somalia in Africa— and killed more than 250,000 people across those regions.

Glossary of Earthquake-Related Terms

Aftershock- A seismic earth tremor , usually of a smaller magnitude that often occurs after a larger magnitude earthquake (mainshock). Aftershocks often occur in "swarms" (see: "swarm") and can go on for a period of days and even months in the same region where preceding earthquake took pace, decreasing in frequency over time.

Amplitude-is the amount of time a seismic wave (created by the energy released by opposing tectonic plate forces) moves through the ground, as measured between the peak and depression of the wave.

Crust-The Earth's outermost layer.

Cryoseism –Also known as "frost quakes," a cryoseism is a cold weather -related geological phenomenon whereby the ground expands and eventually cracks due to the expansion of ice and cold water in embedded in the surrounding soil. This cracking can often result in the creation of small or moderate-sized fissures in the surrounding ground, and is sometimes accompanied by a loud audible explosive noise or "boom." Although not a true tectonic event, a cryoseism can create small seismic waves in the earth that can be measured by nearby seismographs.

Displacement (ground)- is the movement of the ground along geologic faults. This movement often creates violent vertical and horizontal disruptions in the earth strong enough to cause fissures and breakage of roadways, severely damage and/or destroy buildings, and cause severe misalignment of railways, to name a few possible effects within the affected earthquake region. Additionally, more subtle ground displacements also can occur before, during and after an earthquake, and at significant distances from a quake's epicenter.

Earthquake-The sometimes violent shaking of the Earth caused by the sudden release of seismic energy by the opposing movement of rocky tectonic plates deep within the Earth. The energy produces seismic waves that travel outward in all directions from the point of initial rupture. It is these waves that shake the ground as they pass by.

Earthquake swarm-A series of major or minor earthquakes, occurring in a limited area and time.

Epicenter- is the point on the Earth's surface directly above the hypocenter of an earthquake. For all intents and purposes, it is the focal point on the earth's surface where an earthquake's seismic waves emanate.

Fault (earthquake)-A break in the Earth along which movement occurs, usually along two (or more) tectonic plates. The sudden movement of plates along a fault is what produces earthquakes.

Focus (Point of)-That exact (or estimated) point within the Earth from which the seismic waves that create earthquakes originate.

The No-Nonsense Guide To Earthquake Safety

Foreshock-is a seismic small tremor (or series of tremors) that commonly precedes a larger earthquake (or mainshock) anywhere from a few minutes up to a few weeks beforehand. Foreshocks generally originate in or near the rupture zone of a larger (impending) earthquake.

Hypocenter-The exact (or calculated) location of the focus point of an earthquake.

Intensity-is the estimated severity (by way of the observational effects) of ground shaking in a particular area or region. An earthquake's intensity is usually estimated from descriptions of damage to buildings and the local terrain, much like the Enhanced Fujita Scale is used in tornado intensity measurement. The intensity of an earthquake is often—but not always—found to be greatest near the epicenter, and is ranked using the Modified Mercalli Scale (see Mercalli Scale).

Liquification (ground)-occurs when the ground becomes water-saturated during an earthquake, and temporarily loses strength and a substantial amount of its cohesion.

Love wave-A type of surface-based seismic wave that results in the horizontal motion of the ground that travels in the direction of its origin point.

Magnitude-A measurable expression of the total energy released by an earthquake. An earthquake's magnitude is determined by measuring seismic wave waves on seismographs, and is expressed in number values corresponding to a logarithmic numerical scale (see Richter Scale).

Mainshock - (see: "earthquake").

Mantle-The zone of semi-molten rock in the Earth's interior that lies between the crust and the Earth's core. The mantle is approximately 1,740 miles (2,900 km) thick.

Micro-earthquakes-Earthquakes with magnitude of about 2.0 or less on the Richter Scale that are generally not felt by the majority of individuals. Micro-earthquakes (such as cryoseisms) are usually recorded only on local seismographs.

Modified Mercalli Intensity Scale-is the numerical ranking scale commonly used to rank the intensity of earthquakes based on the damage produced (the effect of an earthquake on the Earth's surface is known as earthquake *intensity*). The intensity scale subjectively measures the physical responses and effects of earthquakes such as their ability to awakening individuals, the movement of loose objects, and physical damage to structures, and potential for total destruction. The Modified Mercalli Scale is made up of 12 levels of intensity, ranging from imperceptible shaking to catastrophic destruction, with each level given a designated Roman numeral (from I to XII).

P waves-are the fastest seismic waves produced by an earthquake. They oscillate the ground back and forth along the direction of wave travel.

Plate tectonics – is a widely accepted theory that attempts to explain the movement and the interaction of the Earth's various subterranean rocky plates .

Rayleigh wave-is a type of seismic surface wave results in elliptical (i.e., rolling) motion of the ground at the Earth's surface. Rayleigh waves are the slowest, largest and most destructive wave type produced in an earthquake.

Richter Magnitude Scale-is the logarithmic-based numerical scale used to measure the absolute strength of an earthquake. On the Richter Scale, the magnitude of an earthquake is expressed in whole numbers and decimal fractions. For example, a magnitude 5.3 might be computed for a moderate earthquake, and a strong earthquake might be rated as magnitude 6.3. Because of the logarithmic basis of the scale, each whole number increase in magnitude represents a tenfold increase in measured amplitude; as an estimate of energy, each whole number step in the magnitude scale corresponds to the release of about 31 times more energy than the amount associated with the preceding whole number value.

S waves-Also known as "Secondary" or "shear" waves, S waves are a particular type of seismic wave that rolls the ground perpendicular (up and down) to the direction of its travel. Because liquids will not sustain shear stresses, S waves will not travel through liquids like water, molten rock, or the Earth's outer core.

Seiche-is the disruption of water in a (primarily) land-locked body of water such as a lake or bay produced by earthquakes. Similar to a tsunami (see tsunami) in the open sea/ocean, seiches can be characterized as the sloshing of water in an enclosing basin.

Seismic waves-are the vibrational disturbances in the Earth produced by the energy released from the violent interactions of tectonic plates deep within the Earth. Seismic waves are recorded and measured on instruments called seismographs (see seismographs).

Seismogram-A graph showing the motion of the ground over a period of time. This motion is represented as a series of vacillating lines on seismogram readouts.

Seismograph-A sensitive scientific instrument calibrated to detect and record ground vibrations too small to be perceived by human beings. Seismographs are used to measure and determine the magnitude of an earthquake

Seismologist-is a scientist who studies earthquakes.

Site-effects-the localized geological conditions that tend to impact the general impact of an earthquake

Surface waves-are the general group of 2 specific seismic wave types that move over the surface of the Earth during an earthquake. Each specific type of surface wave has a particular attribute that distinguishes it from the other type in the group. Rayleigh waves and Love waves are types of surface waves.

Tectonic-is a geological term given to scientific studies pertaining to the geological forces involved in the formation, structure, movement, and/or general attributes of the Earth's crust.

The No-Nonsense Guide To Earthquake Safety

Tectonic plates-are the interconnected layers of the uppermost portion of the Earth's mantle that covers the Earth's surface; this includes the layer of earth that makes up the ocean bottoms. Because the earth is not composed of a single stationary continuous layer of rock, tectonic plates tend to interact with each other as they move (very slowly) over the semi-liquid layer of the heated inner-mantle region. It is when these plate interactions result in violent movements that earthquakes occur.

Tsunami-is a large, rapidly moving series of ocean waves triggered by a major disturbance of the ocean floor, which is usually caused by an earthquake but sometimes can be produced by an underwater landslide or a volcanic eruption. Tsunami waves can travel across the open ocean at speeds of between 300-500 mph (482 -804 km/h), but their wave heights are usually only a few inches/centimeters. As they approach shallow water near a coast, tsunami waves travel more slowly, but their wave heights may increase by a factor of many feet/meters, and thus they can become very destructive.

Volcanic earthquakes- are earthquakes are directly associated with geological forces and various pressures associated with magma movement of an active volcano.

The No-Nonsense Guide To Earthquake Safety

Appendix A:

Federal Emergency Management Agency (FEMA) contact information by region

As an extensive government agency, FEMA administrative resources (as well as contact information) have been somewhat decentralized. This is to say that, in order to expedite any assistance to local and state governments (and to limit the potential for bureaucratic confusion), FEMA was divided into regional offices that oversee regional "zones." These *Regional Operations Offices* serve as the arms of the central agency's headquarters (located in Washington D.C.) and through which all policy, managerial, resource and administrative actions effecting coordination between headquarters are initiated.

Region	Location	States Serving
Region I	Boston, MA	CT, MA, ME, NH, RI, VT
Region II	New York, NY	NJ, NY, PR, USVI
Region III	Philadelphia, PA	DC, DE, MD, PA, VA, WV
Region IV	Atlanta, GA	AL, FL, GA, KY, MS, NC, SC, TN
Region V	Chicago, IL	IL, IN, MI, MN, OH, WI
Region VI	Denton, TX	AR, LA, NM, OK, TX

The No-Nonsense Guide To Earthquake Safety

Region	Location	States Serving
Region VII	Kansas City, MO	IA, KS, MO, NE
Region VIII	Denver, CO	CO, MT, ND, SD, UT, WY
Region IX	Oakland, CA	AZ, CA, HI, NV, GU, AS, CNMI, RMI, FM
Region X	Bothell, WA	AK, ID, OR, WA

The No-Nonsense Guide To Earthquake Safety

Contact:

FEMA Region I
99 High St.
Boston, MA 02110
1-877-336-2734
Email

Federal Region II
26 Federal Plaza
New York, NY 10278-0002
Telephone: (212) 680-3600
FEMA-R2-ExternalAffairs@fema.dhs.gov

Puerto Rico and Virgin Islands

Mailing address:
Carribean Division
PO Box 70105
San Juan PR 00936-0105

Physical address:
New San Juan Office Bldg
159 Calle Chardon, 6th Floor
Hato Rey, PR 00918
Telephone: (787) 296-3500

FEMA Region III
One Independence Mall, 6th Floor
615 Chestnut Street
Philadelphia, PA 19106-4404
(215) 931-5500

FEMA Region IV
Federal Emergency Management Agency
3003 Chamblee Tucker Road

Atlanta, GA 30341
Office: 770-220-5200
Fax Number: 770-220-5230

FEMA Region V
Federal Emergency Management Agency
536 South Clark Street, 6th Floor
Chicago, IL 60605
(312) 408-5500

FEMA Region VI
Federal Emergency Management Agency
FRC 800 North Loop 288
Denton, TX 76209-3698
E-Mail: FEMA-R6-RRCC-PrivateSector@fema.dhs.gov
Tribal Affairs
E-Mail Norma.Reyes@fema.dhs.gov
Telephone: 940-898-5233

FEMA Region VII or Federal Emergency Management Agency
9221 Ward Parkway, Suite 300
Kansas City, MO. 64114-3372
Telephone: (816) 283-7061
Tribal Contact
E-mail: jonathan.weinberg@fema.dhs.gov
Telephone: (816) 809-4128

FEMA Region VIII or Federal Emergency Management Agency
Federal Emergency Management Agency
Denver Federal Center
Building 710, Box 25267
Denver, CO 80225-0267
(303) 235-4800

FEMA Region IX
1111 Broadway, Oakland, CA 94607
Phone:(510) 627-7140
Pacific Area Office
(808) 851-7900
Southern California Field Office
(626) 431-3000

FEMA Region X or Federal Emergency Management Agency
Federal Regional Center
130 - 228th Street, Southwest
Bothell, WA 98021-8627
(425) 487-4600

Appendix C:
State Offices and Agencies of Emergency Management
U.S.

A

Alabama Emergency Management Agency
5898 County Road 41
P.O. Drawer 2160
Clanton, Alabama 35046-2160
(205) 280-2476
(205) 280-2442 FAX
http://ema.alabama.gov/

Alaska Division of Homeland Security and Emergency Management
P.O. Box 5750
Fort Richardson, Alaska 99505-5750
(907) 428-7000
(907) 428-7009 FAX
http://www.ak-prepared.com/

American Samoa Territorial Emergency Management Coordination
(TEMCO)
American Samoa Government
P.O. Box 1086
Pago Pago, American Samoa 96799
(011)(684) 699-6415
(011)(684) 699-6414 FAX

Arizona Division of Emergency Management
5636 E. McDowell Road
Phoenix, Arizona 85008-3495
(800) 411-2336 | (602) 244-0504
(602) 464-6356 FAX
http://www.dem.azdema.gov/

Arkansas Department of Emergency Management
Bldg. # 9501
Camp Joseph T. Robinson
North Little Rock, Arkansas 72199-9600

The No-Nonsense Guide To Earthquake Safety

(501) 683-6700
(501) 683-7890 FAX
www.adem.arkansas.gov/

C

California Emergency Management Agency
3650 Schriever Avenue
Mather, California 95655
(916) 845-8506
(916) 845-8511 FAXhttp://www.calema.ca.gov/Pages/default.aspx

Colorado Division Homeland Security and Emergency Management
Department of Public Safety
9195 E. Mineral Avenue
Suite 200
Centennial, Colorado 80112
(720) 852-6600
(720) 852-6750 Fax
http://www.dhsem.state.co.us/ or http://www.coemergency.com/

Connecticut Office of Emergency Management
Department of Emergency Management and Homeland Security
25 Sigourney Street 6th floor
Hartford, Connecticut 06106-5042
(860) 256-0800
(860) 256-0815 FAX
www.ct.gov/demhs/

D

Delaware Emergency Management Agency
165 Brick Store Landing Road
Smyrna, Delaware 19977
(302) 659-3362
(302) 659-6855 FAX
http://www.dema.delaware.gov/

District of Columbia Emergency Management Agency
2720 Martin Luther King, Jr. Avenue, S.E.
Second Floor
Washington, D.C. 20032
(202) 727-6161
(202) 673-2290 FAX
http://hsema.dc.gov/

F

Florida Division of Emergency Management

The No-Nonsense Guide To Earthquake Safety

2555 Shumard Oak Blvd.
Tallahassee, Florida 32399-2100
(850) 413-9969
(850) 488-1016 FAX
http://www.floridadisaster.org/index.asp

G

Georgia Emergency Management Agency
935 East Confederate Ave SE
P.O. Box 18055
Atlanta, Georgia 30316-0055
(404) 635-7000
(404) 635-7205 FAX
http://www.gema.state.ga.us/

Guam Homeland Security/Office of Civil Defense
221B ChalanPalasyo
Agana Heights, Guam 96910
Tel:(671)475-9600
Fax:(671)477-3727
http://ghs.guam.gov/

H

Hawaii State Civil Defense
3949 Diamond Head Road
Honolulu, Hawaii 96816-4495
(808) 733-4300
(808) 733-4287 FAX
http://www.scd.hawaii.gov/

I

Idaho Bureau of Homeland Security
4040 Guard Street, Bldg. 600
Boise, Idaho 83705-5004
(208) 422-3040
(208) 422-3044 FAX
http://www.bhs.idaho.gov/

Illinois Emergency Management Agency
2200 S. Dirksen Pkwy.
Springfield, Illinois 62703
Office: (217) 782-2700 or (217) 782-2700
Fax: (217) 557-1978
http://www.state.il.us/iema/

Indiana Department of Homeland Security

The No-Nonsense Guide To Earthquake Safety

Indiana Government Center South
302 West Washington Street, Room E208
Indianapolis, Indiana 46204-2767
Office: (317) 232-3986
Fax: (317) 232-3895
http://www.in.gov/dhs/emermgtngpgm.htm

Indiana State Emergency Management Agency
302 West Washington Street
Room E-208 A
Indianapolis, Indiana 46204-2767
(317) 232-3986
(317) 232-3895 FAX
http://www.in.gov/dhs/index.html

Iowa Homeland Security & Emergency Management Division
7105 NW 70th Ave, Camp Dodge
Building W-4
Johnston, Iowa 50131
(515) 725-3231
(515) 281-3260 FAX
http://www.iowahomelandsecurity.org/

K

Kansas Division of Emergency Management
2800 S.W. Topeka Boulevard
Topeka, Kansas 66611-1287
(785) 274-1409
(785) 274-1426 FAX
http://www.kansastag.gov/kdem_default.asp

Kentucky Emergency Management
EOC Building
100 Minuteman Parkway Bldg. 100
Frankfort, Kentucky 40601-6168
(502) 607-1682 or (800) 255-2587
(502) 607-1614 FAX
http://kyem.ky.gov/Pages/default.aspx

L

Louisiana Office of Emergency Preparedness
7667 Independence Blvd.
Baton Rouge, Louisiana 70806
(225) 925-7500
(225) 925-7501 FAX
http://www.gohsep.la.gov/

M

Maine Emergency Management Agency
#72 State House Station
45 Commerce Drive, Suite #2
Augusta, Maine 04333-0072
(207) 624-4400
(207) 287-3180 (FAX)
http://www.maine.gov/mema/

CNMI Emergency Management Office
Office of the Governor
Commonwealth of the Northern Mariana Islands
P.O. Box 10007
Saipan, Mariana Islands 96950
(670) 322-9529
(670) 322-7743 FAX
http://www.cnmiemo.gov.mp/

National Disaster Management Office
Office of the Chief Secretary
P.O. Box 15
Majuro, Republic of the Marshall Islands 96960-0015
(011)(692) 625-5181
(011)(692) 625-6896 FAX

Maryland Emergency Management Agency
Camp Fretterd Military Reservation
5401 Rue Saint Lo Drive
Reistertown, Maryland 21136
(410) 517-3600
(877) 636-2872 Toll-Free
(410) 517-3610 FAX
http://mema.maryland.gov/Pages/homePreparedness_heat.aspx

Massachusetts Emergency Management Agency
400 Worcester Road
Framingham, Massachusetts 01702-5399
(508) 820-2000
(508) 820-2030 FAX
http://www.mass.gov/eopss/agencies/mema/

Michigan State Police, Emergency Management & Homeland Security Division
Michigan Dept. of State Police
4000 Collins Road
Lansing, Michigan 48909-8136
(517) 333-5042

(517) 333-4987 FAX
http://www.michigan.gov/msp/0,1607,7-123-1593_3507---,00.html

National Disaster Control Officer
Federated States of Micronesia
P.O. Box PS-53
Kolonia, Pohnpei - Micronesia 96941
(011)(691) 320-8815
(001)(691) 320-2785 FAX

Minnesota Homeland Security and Emergency Management Division
Minnesota Dept. of Public Safety
444 Cedar Street, Suite 223
St. Paul, MN 55101-6223
Office: (651) 201-7400
Fax: (651) 296-0459
https://dps.mn.gov/divisions/hsem/Pages/default.aspx

Mississippi Emergency Management Agency
P.O. Box 5644
Pearl, MS 39288-5644
(601) 933-6362
(800) 519-6362 Toll Free
(601) 933-6800 FAX
http://www.msema.org/

Missouri Emergency Management Agency
2302 Militia Drive
P.O. Box 116
Jefferson City, Missouri 65102
(573) 526-9100
(573) 634-7966 FAX
http://sema.dps.mo.gov/

JFHQ-MT
Montana Division of Disaster & Emergency Services
1956 Mt Majo Street
PO BOX 4789
Fort Harrison, Montana 59636-4789
(406) 841-3911
(406) 841-3965 FAX

http://www.dma.mt.gov/des/

N

Nebraska Emergency Management Agency
1300 Military Road
Lincoln, Nebraska 68508-1090
(402) 471-7421

(402) 471-7433 FAX
http://www.nema.ne.gov/index.shtml

Nevada Division of Emergency Management
2478 Fairview Dr
Carson City, Nevada 89701
(775) 687-0300
(775) 687-0330FAX
http://dem.nv.gov/

Governor's Office of Emergency Management
State Office Park South
33 Hazen Dr
Concord, New Hampshire 03305
(603) 271-2231
(603) 271-3609 FAX
http://www.nh.gov/safety/divisions/hsem/

New Jersey State Police
New Jersey Office of Emergency Management
P.O. Box 7068, River RD
West Trenton, New Jersey 08628-0068
(609) 882-2000 ext 2700 Monday to Friday
(609) 963-6900 Emergency
(609) 963-6208 Mitigation
(609) 963-6992 State Training Officer
(609) 671-0160 Fax
http://www.ready.nj.gov/

New Mexico Department of Homeland Security
and Emergency Management (DHSEM)
13 Bataan Boulevard
P.O. Box 27111
Santa Fe, New Mexico 87502
(505) 476-9600
(505) 476-9635 Emergency
(505) 476-9695 FAX
http://www.nmdhsem.org/

New York State Emergency Management Office
1220 Washington Avenue
Building 22, Suite 101
Albany, New York 12226-2251
(518) 292-2275
(518) 322-4978 FAX
http://www.dhses.ny.gov/oem/

North Carolina Division of Emergency Management - Main Office
1636 Gold Star Drive
4236 Mail Service Center

Raleigh, N.C. 27607-3371
(919) 825-2500
Emergency Management 24-Hour Operations 1-800-858-0368
https://www.ncdps.gov/Index2.cfm?a=000003,000010

North Dakota Department of Emergency Services
P.O. Box 5511
Bismarck, North Dakota 58506-5511
(701) 328-8100
(701) 328-8181 FAX
http://www.nd.gov/des/

O

Ohio Emergency Management Agency
2855 West Dublin-Granville Road
Columbus, Ohio 43235-2206
Office: (614) 889-7150
Fax: (614) 889-7183
http://ema.ohio.gov/

Oklahoma Department of Emergency Management
2401 Lincoln Blvd Suite C51
Oklahoma City, Oklahoma 73105
(405) 521-2481
(405) 521-4053 FAX
http://www.ok.gov/OEM/

Oregon Emergency Management
Department of State Police
3225 State St
Salem, Oregon 97309-5062
(503) 378-2911
(503) 373-7833 FAX
http://www.oregon.gov/OMD/OEM/Pages/index.aspx

P

Palau NEMO Coordinator
Office of the President
P.O. Box 100
Koror, Republic of Palau 96940
(011)(680) 488-2422
(011)(680) 488-3312

Pennsylvania Emergency Management Agency
2605 Interstate Drive
Harrisburg PA 17110-9463
(717) 651-2001
(717) 651-2040 FAX

The No-Nonsense Guide To Earthquake Safety

http://www.pema.state.pa.us/portal/server.pt/community/pema_home/4463

Puerto Rico Emergency Management Agency
P.O. Box 966597
San Juan, Puerto Rico 00906-6597
(787) 724-0124
(787) 725-4244 FAX
http://www2.pr.gov/Directorios/Pages/InfoAgencia.aspx?PRIFA=021

R

Rhode Island Emergency Management Agency
645 New London Ave
Cranston, Rhode Island 02920-3003
(401) 946-9996
(401) 944-1891 FAX
http://www.riema.ri.gov/

S

South Carolina Emergency Management Division
2779 Fish Hatchery Road
West Columbia South Carolina 29172
(803) 737-8500
(803) 737-8570 FAX
http://www.scemd.org/

South Dakota Division of Emergency Management
118 West Capitol
Pierre, South Dakota 57501
(605) 773-3231
(605) 773-3580 FAX
http://dps.sd.gov/emergency_services/emergency_management/

T

Tennessee Emergency Management Agency
3041 Sidco Drive
Nashville, Tennessee 37204-1502
(615) 741-0001
(615) 242-9635 FAX
http://www.tnema.org/

Texas Division of Emergency Management
5805 N. Lamar
PO BOX 4087
Austin, Texas 78773-0220
(512) 424-2138
(512) 424-2444 or 7160 FAX

The No-Nonsense Guide To Earthquake Safety

http://www.txdps.state.tx.us/dem/

U

Utah Division of Emergency Services and Homeland Security
1110 State Office Building
P.O. Box 141710
Salt Lake City, Utah 84114-1710
(801) 538-3400
(801) 538-3770 FAX
http://publicsafety.utah.gov/emergencymanagement/

V

Vermont Emergency Management Agency
Department of Public Safety
Waterbury State Complex
103 South Main Street
Waterbury, Vermont 05671-2101
(802) 244-8721
(800) 347-0488
(802) 244-8655 FAX
http://dps.vermont.gov/

Virgin Islands Territorial Emergency Management - VITEMA
2-C Contant, A-Q Building
Virgin Islands 00820
(340) 774-2244
(340) 774-1491

Virginia Department of Emergency Management
10501 Trade Court
Richmond, VA 23236-3713
(804) 897-6500
(804) 897-6556 FAX
http://www.vaemergency.gov/

W

State of Washington Emergency Management Division
Building 20, M/S: TA-20
Camp Murray, Washington 98430-5122
(253) 512-7000
(800) 562-6108
(253) 512-7200 FAX
http://www.emd.wa.gov/

West Virginia Office of Emergency Services
Building 1, Room EB-80 1900 Kanawha Boulevard, East

The No-Nonsense Guide To Earthquake Safety

Charleston, West Virginia 25305-0360
(304) 558-5380
(304) 344-4538 FAX
http://www.dhsem.wv.gov/Pages/default.aspx
Wisconsin Emergency Management
2400 Wright Street
P.O. Box 7865
Madison, Wisconsin 53707-7865
Phone: (608) 242-3232
Fax: (608) 242-3247
http://emergencymanagement.wi.gov/

Wyoming Homeland Security Training Program
1556 Riverbend Drive
Douglas WY 82633
(307) 358-1920
(307) 358-0994 FAX
http://wyohomelandsecurity.state.wy.us/

Appendix C:
Provincial Offices and Agencies of Emergency Management
Canada

The following list comprises the provincial and territorial emergency management organizations (EMOs) for Canada. These EMOs are responsible for granting administrative, logistical support and assistance, as well as other needed resources to local governments in times of emergencies such as tornadoes.

Alberta
Alberta Emergency Management Agency
Telephone: (780) 422-9000 / Toll-free: 310-0000
www.aema.alberta.ca

British Columbia
British Columbia Provincial Emergency Program
Telephone: (250) 952-4913 / Emergency: 1-800-663-3456
www.pep.bc.ca

Manitoba
Manitoba Emergency Measures Organization
Telephone: (204) 945-4772 / Toll-free: 1-888-267-8298
www.manitobaemo.ca

New Brunswick
New Brunswick Emergency Measures Organization
Telephone: (506) 453-2133 / Toll-free 24 Hour line: 1-800-561-4034
www.gnb.ca/cnb/emo-omu

Newfoundland and Labrador
Newfoundland and Labrador Fire and Emergency Services
Telephone: (709) 729-3703
www.ma.gov.nl.ca/ma/fes

Northwest Territories
Northwest Territories Emergency Management Organization
Telephone: (867) 873-7538 / 24 Hour line: (867) 920-2303
www.maca.gov.nt.ca/emergency_management/index.htm

Nova Scotia
Nova Scotia Emergency Management Office

Telephone Toll-free 24 Hour line: 1-866-424-5620
www.gov.ns.ca/emo

Nunavut
Nunavut Emergency Management
Telephone: (867) 975-5403 / Toll-free 24 Hour line: 1-800-693-1666
http://cgs.gov.nu.ca/en/commEmergency.aspx

Ontario
Emergency Management Ontario
Telephone: (416) 314-3723 / Toll-free 24 Hour line: 1-877-314-3723
www.ontario.ca/emo

Prince Edward Island
Prince Edward Island Emergency Measures Organization
Telephone: (902) 894-0385 / After hours: (902) 892-9365
www.peipublicsafety.ca

Quebec
Quebec – Ministère de la sécuritépublique
Telephone (toll-free): 1-866-644-6826
General information (Services Québec): 1-877-644-4545
www.securitepublique.gouv.qc.ca

Saskatchewan
Saskatchewan Emergency Management Organization
Telephone: (306) 787-9563
www.gr.gov.sk.ca/SaskEMO

Yukon
Yukon Emergency Measures Organization
Telephone: (867) 667-5220
Toll free (within the Yukon): 1-800-661-0408
www.community.gov.yk.ca/emo

Appendix D:
Disaster-Relief Organizations and Charities

This following is a partial list of the many disaster-relief and charitable organizations that those affected by tornado emergencies can turn to in times of need. Below is a sample of the most notable of these organizations.

American Red Cross
http://www.redcross.org/find-help

Catholic Charities USA
http://www.catholiccharitiesusa.org/what-we-do/disaster-operations/

Children's Disaster Services (Church of the Brethren)
http://www.brethren.org/cds/

Christian Disaster Response
http://cdresponse.org/

Feeding America
http://feedingamerica.org/need-
help.aspx?s_src=Y14YPDGAA&s_keyword=feedingamerica&s_subsrc=feedingamerica

National Organization for Victim Assistance (NOVA)
http://www.trynova.org/

Salvation Army
http://www.salvationarmyusa.org/

Jewish federations of North America
http://www.jewishfederations.org/

World Vision
http://www.worldvision.org/m/sponsor-a-child/?open&campaign=1193512&cmp=KNC-
1193512&gclid=CI-G67v8pboCFYSd4AodMhgAIA

Appendix E:

Modern Richter Scale & Damage Description

RICHTER SCALE

Magnitude	Description	What it feels like	Frequency
Less than 2.0	Micro	Normally only recorded by seismographs. Most people cannot feel them.	Millions per year.
2.0–2.9	Minor	A few people feel them. No building damage.	Over 1 million per year.
3.0–3.9	Minor	Some people feel them. Objects inside can be seen shaking.	Over 100,000 per year.
4.0–4.9	Light	Most people feel it. Indoor objects shake or fall to floor.	10,000 to 15,000 per year.
5.0–5.9	Moderate	Can damage or destroy buildings not designed to withstand earthquakes. Everyone feels it.	1,000 to 1,500 per year.
6.0–6.9	Strong	Wide spread shaking far from epicenter. Damages buildings.	100 to 150 per year.
7.0–7.9	Major	Wide spread damage in most areas.	10 to 20 per year.
8.0–8.9	Great	Wide spread damage in large areas.	About 1 per year.
9.0–9.9	Great	Severe damage to most buildings.	1 per 5-50 years.
10.0 or over	Massive	Never Recorded.	Never recorded.

Appendix F:
The Basics of (Earthquake-Related) Building Codes

What are Building Codes?

Building codes are legislated and enforced sets of regulations governing the design, construction, alteration, and maintenance of structures. These codes specify the minimum level of requirements to adequately safeguard the health, safety, and welfare of building occupants as they relate to foreseeable and anticipated threats and potential dangers.

Although it would be easy for most local jurisdictions to create individualized sets of codes (based on the general and particular risk factors for each location), most states and local municipalities have opted to legislate and enforce building codes based on the model building codes maintained by the International Code Council (ICC). The ICC's family of International Codes includes:

- **International Building Code (IBC):** Applies to almost all types of new buildings
- **International Residential Code (IRC):** Applies to new one- and two-family dwellings and townhouses of not more than three stories in height
- **International Existing Building Code (IEBC):** Applies to the alteration, repair, addition, or change in occupancy of existing structures

The ICC publishes new editions of the International Codes every three years, and many states and localities have adopted them since the first editions were issued in 2000. In 2000, the three regionally-based model code organizations (BOCA National Code, SBCCI Standard Code, and ICBO Uniform Code) combined together to form the ICC.

Although building codes regulate standards for older as well as new constructions, most localities recognize that from a financial and practical standpoint, it is far easier for property owners and building contractors to retrofit existing buildings—those most likely constructed prior to the implementation of recent earthquake building codes—with new and/or additional seismic-related safety provisions, making them up-to-code. This is more true in earthquake-prone regions such as those in America's West and Northwest regions.

What Seismic Building Codes Can Do

Seismic building codes result in earthquake-*resistant* buildings, but not earthquake-*proof* buildings. Seismic codes are intended to protect people inside buildings by making the wholesale collapse of a dwelling *less likely* (but not improbable). Structures built according to these codes tend to resist minor earthquakes with less damage, while resisting moderate earthquakes with limited structural damage. In many cases, these building codes can result in dwellings that are up-to-code resist severe or major earthquakes without totally collapsing.

Even Code-Compliant Buildings Can Be Damaged

The No-Nonsense Guide To Earthquake Safety

As stated, earthquake-resistant buildings are not earthquake-proof. This is to say even dwellings that meet seismic-related codes can be damaged (even conceivably collapse) under a powerful enough earthquake. What's more, the interiors of code-compliant buildings may be extensively damaged, making the building either not fully functional or inhabitable until repairs and clean-up are completed. To limit such damage, many buildings have adopted practices that include properly designing and bracing nonstructural elements.

Newer Buildings are generally Safer than Older Buildings

Because they are built under more advanced codes, newer buildings are usually (but not always) safer than older buildings. Steel-frame high-rises and newer wood-frame low-rise buildings are usually (but not always) the safest structure types. As with most things, there are exceptions to such generalizations. These exceptions are based on individual variables such as the configuration of the building, the quality of construction (as well as the materials used), and the manner in which seismic waves impact a particular building site (site-effect).

Seismic Codes Vary across the United States

The seismic provisions of building codes are based on earthquake hazard maps that show the probabilities of earthquake occurrence as well as intensity in particular areas. Building code requirements reflect the fact that some places are more likely than others to have strong earthquakes. This means that seismic-related building codes in one area may not be as stringent as those in other areas, depending on earthquake probability. For example, standards for seismic-sensitive building codes may be less in Boston than in Los Angeles. Conversely, seismic code requirements in southern Illinois, near the New Madrid seismic zone, are much stricter than in Chicago in the north of the state, which is less likely to have a strong earthquake.

There are three regions within the U.S. that are prone to earthquake activity. These include Charleston, S.C., the five states in the New Madrid/Wabash Valley Seismic Zone, and the Pacific West Coast. Current building codes in South Carolina and in the Pacific West Coast states meet acceptable standards for seismic resistance.

- **CHARLESTON, S.C.** - Charleston and its outlying areas were the site of an earthquake in 1886 that destroyed approximately one-quarter of the city's buildings and killed more than 100 people. The state follows the 2006 edition of the International Codes and has made no amendments to the seismic provisions, which are considered adequate protections. The state first adopted a statewide code and mandatory enforcement in July 2003, which equates to a limited inventory of code compliant structures. The latest hazard maps have been revised to include offshore faults that may be capable of generating earthquakes, which may increase the chances of an earthquake in the Charleston area.

- **PACIFIC WEST COAST** - The Pacific West Coast includes California, Oregon, and Washington. All three states have mandatory statewide building codes in place in accordance with the 2006 version of the International Codes. Each of the states has passed amendments that exceed the ICC codes to make the seismic requirements more stringent. The building standards in place in this region of the country are more reflective of the latest and best available science.

- **NEW MADRID ZONE/WABASH VALLEY** - The New Madrid/Wabash Valley Seismic Zone was the site of three major earthquakes and a series of aftershocks from 1811-1812, which are considered the most intense inter-plate earthquakes to have occurred in recorded U.S. history.

    This fault zone crosses the states of Arkansas, Illinois, Indiana, Kentucky, Mississippi, Missouri, and Tennessee. It is apparent from reviewing the status of the building codes in this region that several states do not have adequate code coverage and/or code enforcement in place. This is despite agreement among most scientists that there is a 90 percent probability of an earthquake of a magnitude between 6 and 7 occurring in this region in the next 50 years, according to the U.S. Geological Survey.The apparent earthquake risk combined with the large geographic area and population that would be affected and the lack of appropriate building codes to reduce earthquake damage make this a region of great concern to the Insurance Institute for Business & Home Safety (IBHS).

On Feb. 10, 2010, a quake of magnitude 3.8 shook northern Illinois. The quake was felt in Georgia, Illinois, Indiana, Iowa, Kentucky, Michigan, Ohio, Tennessee and Wisconsin. People reported that dishes rattled, buildings swayed and glass shower doors shook violently. While this quake was not attributed to the New Madrid fault, it demonstrates the effects of even a mild earthquake. By comparison, the earthquake in Haiti registered 7.0, making its magnitude 1,600 times greater than a quake of magnitude 3.8.

Older Buildings Are Frequently Not Seismically Safe

Generally speaking, seismic codes did not come into wide use in the eastern U.S. until the early or mid 1990s. In the western U.S., seismic codes made substantial improvements in construction as early as the mid 1970s. Buildings constructed prior to these respective dates in each area are probably not seismically safe. Retrofitting buildings to achieve seismic resistance is possible, but often costly, so choices must be made about which buildings are most important to fix. Buildings with high occupancy, critical response services (fire, police, hospitals), and vulnerable populations (schools, nursing homes) are most likely to be built to code. Likewise, structures related to utilities and an area's infrastructure will also likely be built (or reinforced) up-to-code (otherwise, earthquake damage to critical structures and institutions necessary to maintain crucial services could lead to a greater life loss, larger economic loss and greater social disruption, and slow community response in the event of an earthquake).

Codes Change over Time

The model upon which many state and local building codes (and their seismic provisions) are based on are revised every 3 years, based on advancements in engineering and effective building designs.

Appendix G:
Earthquake Insurance Primer

Throughout the world, more than a million earthquakes occur every year, which is the equivalent of 1 every 30 seconds, according to the Center for Earthquake Research and Information. Most of these earthquakes are in fact micro-earthquakes—those with a magnitude too small (or their locations too remotes) to be felt by humans

In the U.S., earthquakes pose a significant risk to 75 million Americans in 39 states out of the 50 states (and territories), according to the U.S. Geological Survey. In the period between the years 2002 to 2012, earthquakes of magnitude of 4.0 or greater on the Richter scale occurred in 23 U.S. states. On the whole, earthquakes of a magnitude 6.5 or greater cause the greatest number of property damage, injuries, and fatalities.

Along with increased concerns about personal safety in regard to earthquakes, individuals and homeowners—especially those in earthquake-prone regions—might want to consider purchasing earthquake insurance to protect against financial loss incurred by earthquake damage. Most standard home- and property-owners' insurance policies generally do not cover financial losses caused by earthquake damage, however additional coverage can be purchased in most states.

How to Map Earthquake Odds

While it's nearly impossible to predict where the next quake will hit, homeowners can get a rough idea of their risk by using seismic hazard maps from the U.S. Geological Survey. As one would expect, the biggest high-risk zone is along the West Coast in California, Oregon and Washington. But there are also hot spots in Nevada, Utah and Wyoming. Further east, a major hazard area called the New Madrid Seismic Zone straddles parts of Illinois, Missouri, Arkansas, Tennessee and Kentucky. South Carolina has its own red zone. And much of Hawaii and Alaska are also rated high risk.

Know What's Covered

Generally speaking, earthquake insurance covers damages to the home or its contents that are caused by earthquakes. This might include collapsed walls or valuable contents that were destroyed inside the house.

Some other earthquake-related damages might not be covered. For example, damages or losses due to flooding that result from an earthquake, whether caused by tidal wave, tsunami, or otherwise, may not be covered by earthquake insurance. Every policy will cover some damages but not others, so it's essential to read the policy thoroughly. Additionally, possessions of particular value, such as collectibles may require supplemental or individual coverage.

Premiums and Deductibles

As with any insurance policy, the cost of earthquake coverage is based on the probability of earthquake damage to property, based on its location in and/or around an active earthquake zone. Insurance *premiums* (what one pays) for earthquake insurance vary widely based on a number of factors. The location of a particular property is the primary consideration (this is because coverage in high-risk areas is much more expensive than in areas that have never had a significant quake). Other factors that are taken into consideration in calculating premiums include the age of the dwelling, the type of construction used in the dwelling, the value of the property/dwelling, the type of home (or building) to be covered, and the amount of the *deductable* (initial out-of-pocket expenses of payments).

The put these factors into context, wood-framed houses, for example, tend to withstand earthquakes better than brick homes, while many newer homes in earthquake hazard areas use updated with seismic-focused construction methods to make them more quake-resistant. At the same time, insurance deductibles are usually calculated as a percentage of a home or property's value. In most areas, the deductible is 10% or more of the property's overall value). So the value of a solid, recently-constructed wood-frame $100,000 home in a recognized moderate-earthquake-zone area may cover damages over $10,000 (or after the first $10,000 is paid by the homeowner). Those factors impact a policy's premiums.

Appendix H:
The Future of Earthquake Prediction

Simply put, at our current level of understanding, human beings cannot actually predict when an earthquake will occur. However, thanks in large part to the increase of our overall understanding of plate tectonics (the movement of the plates within the Earth and the location of fault zones) and related geologic science, scientists *can* predict where major earthquakes are likely to occur based on the. Additionally, scientist have learned to probability-related predictions as to when earthquakes might occur in a given area by examining the history of earthquakes in the region and detecting where pressure is building along fault lines. For example, if a region has experienced a series of magnitude 7 or larger quakes during the past 200 years, scientists are able to calculate the probability of another magnitude 7 quake occurring in the next 50 years at a maximum level of 50%. However, because earthquake prediction is still in its relative infancy, such "predictions" may not turn out to be reliable because, when strain is released along one part of a fault system, it may actually increase strain on another part.

But scientists have had more success predicting aftershocks, based on extensive research of aftershock patterns. Seismologists can make a good guess of how an earthquake originating along one fault will cause additional earthquakes in connected faults. There are, however, some promising advancements being made in ascertaining information on (possible) environmental changes that may serve as indicators of an impending earthquake.

One of these areas of study is the relationship between magnetic and electrical charges in rock material and earthquakes. Some scientists have hypothesized that these electromagnetic fields change in a certain way just before an earthquake. Seismologists are also studying gas seepage and the tilting of the ground as warning signs of earthquakes. In 2009, for example, a technician at Italy's National Institute for Nuclear Physics claimed that he was able to predict the L'Aquila earthquake by measuring the radon gas seeping from the Earth's crust. His findings, however remain controversial.

There are also hints that some earthquake faults themselves might provide a level of warning signals in the days and months before a large earthquake, according to preliminary research. These possible indicators range from tiny shocks along the fault, which may be beyond the limit of detection by today's seismic monitors, to earthquakes large enough to rattle houses. The common thread is that the final "rip"— the actual mainshoock/earthquake—strikes at or near the site of the smaller, earlier breaks. But again, drawing and proving an actual link between these earthquake precursors and larger earthquakes is controversial in the realm of seismology. While many laboratory studies indicate there may seismic warning signals to watch for, not all earthquakes have such indicating foreshocks. Still, geoscientists hope that by better understanding what happens before an earthquake, they may one day have a means of warning the public of increased earthquake risk.

Appendix I
Animal Prediction & Earthquakes

Since the beginning of recorded history, earthquakes have sewn fear and awe into a great many human beings, particularly those who have a history of being affected by their occasional occurrences. And for centuries, these same human beings, in their striving to both understand and predict the onset of these seismic events, have documented observational changes in animal behaviors prior to earthquakes. For a long time, cases of unusual pre-earthquake animal behaviors were attributed to the natural, but unexplainable powers that animals have that allow them to sense oncoming natural disasters.

This belief in the apparent predictive abilities of some animals would go on to gain general acceptance, particularly in more traditional societies. According to Japanese myth, the cause of earthquakes is the giant catfish *Namazu* who lives buried in the underground. By moving his tail he can shake the entire earth and unfortunately he loves to cause trouble and havoc. However in early traditions the catfish also acts as premonition of danger, warning people from an imminent catastrophe or by swallowing dangerous water-dragons prevents further catastrophes. Before the earthquakes of *Edo* (modern Tokyo) in 1855 and later in 1923 apparently catfishes acted weird, displaying increased activity and swimming to the surface of ponds and rivers.

In China, changes in animal behavior was not only observed, but taken as semi-reliable method to be put to use in predicting earthquakes in that earthquake-prone region of the world. For example, in 1975 Chinese officials ordered the evacuation of Haicheng, a city with one million people, just days before a 7.3-magnitude quake. Only a small portion of the population was hurt or killed. If the city had not been evacuated, it is estimated that the number of fatalities and injuries could have exceeded 150,000.

The Haicheng case set a precedent in the establishment of the notion that earthquakes might be predictable. The Chinese have continued to look at animal behavior as an aid to earthquake prediction. They have had several notable successes and also a few false alarms. But as Chinese scientists have discovered, not all earthquakes cause unusual animal behavior while others do. As a result of this reality, an evidentiary link between a consistent and reliable behavior pattern prior to seismic events, and a mechanism explaining how this works still eludes us. And while scientists in both China and Japan have engaged in the majority of the research pursuant to this general issue, researchers from other parts of the globe, including the U.S. have begun to explore studying this issue.

Scientists in both the U.S. and Europe for example, have postulated several theories as to why it appears that some animals might engage in strange behavior prior to an earthquake. Among the possible explanations is that many animals with more keen senses might be able to feel seismic P wave seconds before [the] S wave arrives. Another possible explanation is that animals may sense chemical changes in groundwater that occur when an earthquake is about to strike. This is based on the assumption, of course, that certain animals that live in or near groundwater are highly sensitive to any changes in surrounding rocks, or the chemical makeup in the water itself. Researchers began exploring this possible link chemical/water link after seeing a colony of toads abandon its pond in L'Aquila, Italy, in 2009 - days before a quake. The speculation is the presence of an assumed mechanism whereby stressed rocks in the Earth's crust release charged particles that react with the groundwater—changes detected by water-dwelling animals.

That keener animal' senses enable them to perceive minute changes that might occur in the surrounding environment prior to an earthquake is the basis for why a possible animal earthquake link might in fact exist. For example, it is widely known that snakes and some insects can detect thermal variations based on their infrared vision. Physicist Friedemann T. Freund demonstrated in 1993 that rocks under tension emit infrared radiation and infrared anomalies were also recorded by a NASA *Terra* satellite before the magnitude 7.9 Bhuj India earthquake on January 21, 2001. There is a suspicion that these creatures might be able to sense accumulating stresses applied to rocks by movements within the earth.

It seems however reasonable to assume that animals show reactions to variations of their environment caused by an earthquake or the tectonic processes that can cause an earthquake. For this reason, it is best to take heed of any noted and unusual changes in animal behavior which cannot be explained away, especially if such changes take place in earthquake-prone regions.

Index

References

"After an Earthquake." *Federal Emergency Management Agency (FEMA)* website. Retrieved 12 January 2014.

"*Animals & Earthquake Prediction.* " United States Geological Survey website. Retrieved 23 January 2013.

Appell, David. "Danger Signals," *New Scientist* 174, no. 2347 (June 15, 2002): 12. Main Serials Q1 .N52.
 "Basic Disaster Supplies Kit." Updated 5 September 2013 *Ready.gov* website. Retrieved 18 October 2013.

"Big Worldwide Database Aims to Identify Quake Risks, Reduce Deaths," Oskin, Becky. *NBC News* website. Retrieved 11 January 2014.
Bowler, Sue. "Seeing with Seismics," *New Scientist* 172, no. 2316 (November 10, 2001): insert 1-4. Main Serials Q1 .N52.

 "Building Codes." Janurary 25, 2013. *Federal Emergency Management Agency (FEMA)* website. Retrieved 12 January 2014. Retrieved 14 January 2014.

Chester, Roy. "Furnace of Creation, Cradle of Destruction: A Journey to the Birthplace of Earthquakes, Volcanoes, and Tsunamis." AMACOM, 2008

Cicerone, R. D., Ebel, J. E. and Britton, J. "A systematic compilation of earthquake precursors." (2009). Tectonophysics. Accessed May 23, 2013.

Colby, Anne. "What to Keep in Your Earthquake Survival Kits at Home and in the Car." March 17, 2014. LA Times website. Retrieved 29 March 2014.

"During an Earthquake: Indoor Safety." *National Centers For Disease Control (CDC)* website. Retrieved 11 January 2014.

"Earthquakes" *American Red Cross* website. Retrieved 11 January 2014.

"Earthquake Hazards." Earthquake Hazard Program page, the United States Geological Survey website. Retrieved 14 January 2014.

Henao, Luis Andres. "Chile earthquake: Massive Earthquake Causes Landslides, Tsunami, 10 Aftershocks," *Associated Press* / Christian Science Monitor. April 1, 2014

"Historic Earthquakes." United Stated Geological Survey website. Retrieved 10 January 2014.

Hough. Susan. Predicting the Unpredictable: The Tumultuous Science of Earthquake Prediction. Princeton University Press, 2009

Howard, Brian Clark. "Bizarre Earthquake Lights Finally Explained." January 6, 2014. National Geographic Magazine (online). Retrieved 3 February 2014.

Hymon, Steve. "Designing a Subway to Withstand an Earthquake." August 10, 2012. The Source Metro website. Retrieved 10 January 2014.

"Importance of Strong Building Codes in Earthquake-Prone States." Disaster Safety.org website. Retrieved 14 January 2014.

Jones, Nicola. "The Quake Machine," *New Scientist* 170, no. 2297 (June 30, 2001): 34-37. Main Serials Q1 .N52.

Jones, Nicola. "Warning! 25 Seconds Till Disaster Strikes," *New Scientist* 175, no. 2357 (August 24, 2002): 19. Main Serials Q1 .N52.

Kellis-Borok, Vladimir. "Earthquake Prediction: State-of-the-art and Emerging Possibilities," *Annual Review of Earth and Planetary Science* 30 (2002): 1-33. Main Serials QE1 .A55.

Kirschvink, J.L. "Earthquake Prediction by Animals: Evolution and Sensory Perception." (2000). Bulletin of the Seismological Society of America. Retrieved 28 November 2013.

The No-Nonsense Guide To Earthquake Safety

Kristof, Kathy. "Earthquake Insurance: 8 things You Need To Know." CBS News *MoneyWatch*. 7 November 2011. *CBS News* website. Retrieved 28 November 2013.

Kumagai, Jean. "In Japan Earthquake, Early Warnings Helped." March 15, 2011. *Japanese Meteorological Agency* website. Retrieved 9 January 2014.

Marone, Chris. "Stressed to Quaking Point," *Nature* 419, no. 6902 (September 5, 2002): 32. Main Serials Q1.N28.

Mason, Betty. "5 Most Dangerous U.S. Earthquake Hot Spots Beyond California." October 28 2010. Wired magazine online. Retrieved 3 February 2014.

Murray, Jessica and Paul Segall. "Testing Time-predictable Earthquake Recurrence by Direct Measurement of Strain Accumulation and Release," *Nature* 419, no. 6904 (September 19, 2002): 287-291. Main Serials Q1.N28.

Musson, R. *The Million Death Quake.* (2012). Macmillan.

"Preparing Your Earthquake Survival Kit." Staff Writer. January 13, 2014. LA Times website. Retrieved 2 February 2014.

Sammis, C. G. and D. Sornette. "Positive Feedback, Memory, and the Predictability of Earthquakes," *Proceedings of the National Academy of Sciences of the United States of America* 99, no. 4 (February 19, 2002 supp1): 2501-2508. Main Serials Q11 .N26.

Stokstad, Erik. "Deep Quakes Slow but Very Steady," *Science* 295, no. 5564 (March 29, 2002): 2344-2345. Main Serials Q1 .S35.

Stromberg, Joseph. "Why Do Lights Sometimes Appear in the Sky During An Earthquake?" January 2, 2014. *Smithsonian Magazine* website. Retrieved 2 February 2014.

Wiens, Douglas A. and Nathaniel O. Snider. "Repeating Deep Earthquakes: Evidence for Fault Reactivation at Great Depth," *Science* 293, no. 5534 (August 24, 2001): 1463-1466. Main Serials Q1 .S35.

"What Not to Do During an Earthquake (And Why We Did it Anyway)," Balthazar, Giovanni S. *Delco News Network* website. Retrieved 12 January 2014.

"What To Do Immediately When Shaking Begins." Earthquake Country website. Retrieved 13 January 2014.

"When the ground shakes" brochure published by the Seattle office of Emergency Management. 2013.

The No-Nonsense Guide To Earthquake Safety

Zielinski, Sarah.   "Large Earthquakes Still Possible in the Central United States." January 23, 2014. *Smithsonian Magazine* website. Retrieved 2 February 2014.

Picture Credits

Cover Credits:
United States Geological Survey
http://earthquake.usgs.gov/earthquakes/states/events/1906_04_18_pics_1.php

The London Telegraph
http://www.telegraph.co.uk/earth/earthnews/8421290/Blackpool-earthquake-the-Richter-scale-explained.html

Alaska Earthquake Information Center
 http://www.aeic.alaska.edu/quakes/Alaska_1964_earthquake.html

How It Works.com
http://www.howitworksdaily.com/environment/massive-marine-mountains/

National Geographic
http://environment.nationalgeographic.com/environment/natural-disasters/earthquake-profile/

P. 3
The LondonTelegraph.uk

p. 4

The No-Nonsense Guide To Earthquake Safety

http://www.subdude-site.com/WebPages_Local/Blog/topics/energy/earthCrustThin_limitedOil/energy_earthCrustThin_limitedOil.htm

p. 5
Daily Galaxy.com
http://www.dailygalaxy.com/my_weblog/2011/07/new-force-driving-earths-tectonic-plates-discovered.html

How it Works.com
http://www.howitworksdaily.com/environment/massive-marine-mountains/

p. 7
SMS Tsunami Warning.com
http://www.sms-tsunami-warning.com/pages/mercalli-scale#.U4pbiPldWSo

p. 8
BBC.uk

p. 10
Accuweather.com
p. 13
Earth Magazine website
http://www.earthmagazine.org/article/benchmarks-hebgen-lake-earthquake-and-landslide

p. 14
Wikipedia Commons

p. 20
University of California, Berkley website

p. 21
IRIS & The University of Portland website

p. 23
Smithsonian Online and the United States Geological Survey website.

p. 26
Crossroads website
http://xrds.acm.org/article.cfm?aid=1247243

p. 28

The No-Nonsense Guide To Earthquake Safety

Idaho State University website

http://geology.isu.edu/wapi/envgeo/EG5_earthqks/eg_mod5.htm

Japanese Meteorological Agency website

p. 29
Japanese Meteorological Agency website

p. 33
National Geographic
http://news.nationalgeographic.com/news/2014/01/140106-earthquake-lights-earthquake-prediction-geology-science

p. 34
United States Geological Survey website

p. 39
LA Times Online
http://www.latimes.com/news/local/earthquakes/la-me-earthquake-checklist-g,0,3391133.graphic#ixzz2zom3B1qK

p. 41
Waikato Region Emergency Management website

p. 45
The Source Metro.com
http://thesource.metro.net/2012/08/10/designing-a-subway-to-withstand-an-earthquake/

p. 46

p. 47 New York Daily News
http://www.nydailynews.com/news/san-francisco-earthquake-remembered-24-years-gallery-1.1488727?pmSlide=1.1488711

p. 48
http://www.seagrant.umn.edu/superior/processes

The No-Nonsense Guide To Earthquake Safety

Other Books in the No-Nonsense Safety Guide Series

Published By Lulu Books & Beyond The Spectrum

The No-Nonsense Guide To Tornado Safety

• Paperback: 84 pages • Publisher: lulu.com (November 22, 2013) • Language: English • ISBN-10: 1304648648 • ISBN-13: 978-1304648648 • Product Dimensions: 9 x 6 x 0.2 inches • Shipping Weight: 6.4 ounce

The No-Nonsense Guide To Blizzard Safety

The No-Nonsense Guide To Earthquake Safety

• Paperback: 54 pages • Publisher: lulu.com (December 21, 2013) • Language: English • ISBN-10: 9781304709394 • Product Dimensions: 9 x 6 x 0.2 inches • Shipping Weight: 0.28 pounds

The No-Nonsense Guide To Flood Safety.

• Paperback: 60 pages • Publisher: lulu.com (November 22, 2013) • Language: English • ISBN-10: 1304648613 • Product Dimensions: 9 x 6 x 0.2 inches

The No-Nonsense Guide To Hurricane Safety.

• Paperback: 59 pages • Publisher: lulu.com (December 20, 2013) • Language: English • ISBN-10: 9781304733030 • Product Dimensions: 9 x 6 x 0.2 inches

The No-Nonsense Guide To Earthquake Safety

Other upcoming books in the series include: "The No-Nonsense Guide to Fire Safety," and "The No-Nonsense Guide To Automobile Safety."